THE ATHENAEUM

CLUB AND SOCIAL LIFE IN LONDON

1824–1974

HEINEMANN · LONDON

Heinemann Educational Books Ltd

LONDON EDINBURGH MELBOURNE AUCKLAND TORONTO
SINGAPORE HONG KONG KUALA LUMPUR
NAIROBI IBADAN JOHANNESBURG
LUSAKA NEW DELHI

ISBN 0 435 32010 6

First published 1975

Published by
Heinemann Educational Books Ltd
48 Charles Street, London W1X 8AH
Printed and bound in Great Britain by
Richard Clay (The Chaucer Press), Ltd.,
London and Bungay

On 23 May 1974, when the Athenaeum celebrated the one hundred and fiftieth anniversary of its foundation by a Commemoration Dinner, the Club was honoured by the presence in the Chair of HRH the Duke of Edinburgh, Honorary Life Member.

His speech on that occasion, together with that of Lord Morris of Borth-y-Gest who replied on behalf of the Club, are printed on pages 151–158 of this book.

Chapters I–IX are written by Mr. F. R. Cowell, who is grateful to Members for suggestions they have made, and some of them are named; but this does not involve them in responsibility for the text as a whole.

The Appendices were provided by the Librarian Mrs. Roseveare and her assistant.

Contents

List of Illustrations

THE ATHENAEUM

CHAPTER ONE

Origin and Development

Coffee-Houses and Dining-Clubs

When Samuel Johnson defined 'Club' in his famous dictionary, he gave as one of its meanings, 'An assembly of good fellows meeting under certain conditions', putting however another meaning on it by a quotation from Dryden, 'what right has any man to meet in factious clubs to vilify the government?' Charles II felt this so strongly that he tried, unsuccessfully, to close all coffee-houses in 1675. Such a link between Clubs and sedition had a long history reaching back at least to the Roman Republic. But, by the eighteenth century, few would have suspected a *double entendre* in Cowper's verse referring to playing-cards, 'Clubs, typical of strife', although some Clubs merited such a description. Such was the notorious Hell-Fire Club; but one of its prominent members matured to help to found the Society of Dilettanti in 1732, a dining-club whose members gave priceless treasures to the Department of Classical Antiquities of the British Museum.

What led the English to establish social-clubs for gentlemen? One necessary condition was the possession of sufficient wealth, leisure and desire to meet together. These benefits had been provided since the seventeenth century in England by the Elizabethan revolution in agriculture, the growth of population, the development of industry and world trade which that revolution had made possible. In political life two revolutions had resulted in a settled form of government and of social order. Villages grew to be small towns, while some became large. Men were brought together more often, and many had more leisure. Inns, coffee-houses, spas and pleasure gardens all became part of commercial enterprise that sought to profit by catering for the relatively few prosperous gentry and men of business and affairs. Favoured coffee-houses had their regular customers. Dryden and Addison were often to be seen in Will's Coffee-House in Covent Garden. Button's, established by Addison in Russell Street, Covent Garden, was another. Their story has often been recounted. (Hundreds are listed in *London Coffee Houses* by B. Lillywhite, Allen & Unwin, 1963.) Newspapers, magazines, books, all began, especially in the second half of the eighteenth century, to multiply beyond the number that any single individual would acquire, although many people were usually ready to look at those to which they could gain access. Such printed matter became therefore a bait to draw men to inns, taverns and coffee-houses. Proprietors of such establishments as the Star and Garter Hotel in Pall Mall were very ready to give their regular customers every attention. Nevertheless, however frequently *habitués* flocked to their favourite coffee-house to encounter their friends, to make new friends, to read the newspapers, their presence there did not make such places a Club. Anyone could go to them. There were no conditions, no Club rules limiting admission to congenial characters with common interests.

It may seem natural in such circumstances that Clubs should arise, as indeed they did, rapidly, during the first quarter of the nineteenth century. However, in Paris, where all the same conditions were present, where social, literary and cultural life gave a tone and model to the rest of Europe, nothing like the English Club was established. Men met their friends at restaurants such as Beauvilliers or at the Café Turc and after at Antoine's. In the eighteenth century the *salon* flourished, presided over by ladies and providing therefore a mixed social scene that had no real counterpart in England. At the celebrated breakfasts at Holland House in Kensington in the early nineteenth century, Lady Holland's guests were men. Dinner parties for men and women were probably as frequent in the great London houses as in the *hôtels particuliers* of Paris but none developed into the equivalent of the *salons* of the Boulevard Saint-Germain or the Chaussée d'Antin.

That industrious antiquary John Timbs in his entertaining volume *Clubs and Club Life in London* (1872) distinguished between 'Dining-Clubs' and 'Subscription Houses'. In the nineteenth century there were always more 'assemblies of good fellows' meeting regularly and privately in some hospitable tavern than there were in settled Clubs with 'subscription houses' of their own to which none but Members were admitted. Some of the old dining-clubs had a long history. Three of the most eminent, the Royal Society Club, the Society of Dilettanti, and Johnson's literary circle, The Club, antedate all 'subscription houses'. Together with the later (1812) Roxburghe Club they flourish still without their own Clubhouse. They survived because they had their own aims, interests and purposes beyond the conviviality that no doubt also strengthened their fellow-feeling, whereas none of the Clubs depending upon a convivial spirit alone has managed to endure. This contrast so well points to a change in English social and cultural life in the early nineteenth century that a brief reference will not be out of place here to two of the renowned convivial dining-clubs.

One found a chronicler in Walter Arnold who in 1871 celebrated *The Life and Death of the Sublime Society of Beef Steaks from 1735*, with illustrations of the considerable insignia used in its strictly enforced ritual. It became the most distinguished of several Beef Steak Clubs. In the eighteenth century its Members were required to appear in blue coats and buff waistcoats with brass buttons, with the Club's motto, also on the gold rings they had to wear, 'Beef and Liberty'. It was a motto that did not deter the Prince of Wales, the Duke of York and the Duke of Sussex from joining a Club that had also counted as Members Hogarth, George Coleman, Cibber, Wilkes, Garrick, the Duke of Norfolk, and later the Duke of Wellington, Brougham, John Cam Hobhouse, Lord Broughton, Gladstone and others. After 'the Ettrick Shepherd', Hogg, had been a guest he gave a lyrical account of the Club to which he said that the Prince of Wales, later George IV, had to wait three years for admission, but this is probably a misunderstanding. The membership was increased from twenty-four to twenty-five in order to admit him in 1785. The Sublime Society lingered on with a dwindling attendance until the last eighteen nominal Members liquidated it in 1867. It had no building of its own but it had considerable property in engravings, drawings, paintings, silver, glass, chairs and miscellaneous effects including a marble bust of John Wilkes, all of which were sold at Christie's on 7 April 1869 in 131 lots producing £659. A *couteau de chasse* with a handle attributed to Cellini brought £84, the bust of Wilkes £23. Such a forgotten aspect of Club history is worth citing because it shows that some eighteenth-century 'associations of goodfellows' were developing towards the 'subscription house' of the nineteenth century, even upon so slender a basis as a liking for steak, baked potatoes, onions, beetroot, shallots and toasted cheese, washed down by porter, port wine, punch and whisky toddy at a cost of five shillings. The entrance fee, however, was £26. 5s. Of the Members, the Duke of Sussex alone became a Member of the Athenaeum.

One or two gifted, engaging personalities were often sufficient to keep a dining-club in being. A constellation as brilliant as that which Johnson gathered around him in The Club was rare indeed, but talent short of genius would often suffice. Thus that clever versifier Captain Charles Morris became the life and soul of the Sublime Society of Beef Steaks. In their company he vaunted the joys of town life.

In town let me live then, in town let me die
For in truth I can't relish the country, not I,
If one must have a villa in summer to dwell
Oh! give me the sweet shady side of Pall Mall.

He must have looked upon the new Athenaeum with a jaundiced eye after it had cast a different shade upon Pall Mall. When the Athenaeum was founded, he was seventy-nine years old, hardly an age at which men look for a new Club.

Morris had been the 'Sun of the table' at Carlton House whose loss he deplored, and also at Norfolk House. Twenty-four editions of his *Songs Political and Convivial* had appeared by 1830. Many were composed and sung at the Sublime Society who were in complete agreement with his ardent prayer for beef and liberty:

May beef long bless this favoured coast
Where no despotic ruffian
Hath dared a Brazen Bull to roast
With men alive for stuffing
Where never Jove, a tyrant god
Who loves fair maids to purloin
Like a white bull the billows rode
With Madam on his sirloin

'Laugh while you may' was the title of another of his songs, indicating well enough the character of an eminently 'clubbable' man who said:

When the crabbed with spleen would o'ershadow life's scene,
I light up a spark to dispel it;
And if snarlers complain, 'What's this laughing fool's name?'
Next verse of my ballad will tell it.
I'm a brat of old Horace – the song-scribbling Morris
More noted for rhyme than for reason,
One who roars and carouses, makes noise in all houses
And takes all good things in their season.
To this classic of joy, I became when a boy
A pupil most ardent and willing;
And through life as a man, I've stuck fast to this plan
And passed it in flirting and filling.

It is clearly the company and not the stone, marble and splendid architecture that make a Club. This is why the date, 16 February 1824, six years before the Clubhouse opened, is to be celebrated as the origin of the Athenaeum. It was no rollicking affair, such as the Sublime Society of Beef Steaks, or another Beef Steak Club in the Dublin Theatre over which pert, pretty Peg Woffington presided in 1749. The Athenaeum was intended for serious-minded men devoted to the life of the mind; not however in any way exclusive of the lighter side of life.

Another later dining-club with a very distinguished reputation in the nineteenth century was Grillion's, so-called because its Members met either at breakfast or dinner at Grillion's Hotel, No. 20 Albemarle Street until 1860 when Mr. Grillion moved to larger premises, the Clarendon Hotel in Bond Street. Perhaps because most of its Members were peers or their relations, it was regarded as a mark of special social distinction to be a Member. The Club was founded in 1812, but it was not until 1861 that the first Honorary Member was elected. He was George Richmond, the celebrated portrait painter, socially very popular, a Member of The Club and of the Athenaeum since 1856 (under Rule II) to which he bequeathed 'five vast volumes of engravings'.

Little can be gleaned from the privately printed account of its first fifty years (1812–64), *Grillion's Club* (1880), but the recovery of records from 1812–79 led to a splendid new volume in 1914. In 1880 its distinguished Secretaries looked back upon 'fifty years of uninterrupted prosperity, promotive of many generous and enduring friendships, much genial and hearty enjoyment, and instructive intercommunication of valuable knowledge and social interest'. After this high praise, quoted here because it aptly sums up the chief satisfactions that a Club provides, it is surprising to read that in the following year Sir Stratford de Redcliffe broke the record of the Club by dining alone, after which he made a short speech to Mr. Grillion and the waiters that was received with cheers, all the louder, no doubt, because he invited them to drain all the uncorked bottles provided for the absent Members.

Long after the chief of the large 'subscription houses' had first opened their doors, such periodically meeting assemblies of good fellows kept their dining-clubs alive. In 1860 twenty-six such Clubs were meeting at the Thatched House Tavern at the bottom of St. James's Street before they had to look elsewhere when it was demolished in 1863. Among them were the three distinguished still surviving dining-clubs already mentioned: the Royal Society, the Society of Dilettanti and Johnson's The Club.

Some nineteenth-century individualists affected a scorn for Clubs. That 'very odd and very clever' woman, as Sydney Smith referred to Mrs. George Grote, 'the Radical Queen', described how she aided Lord Overstone to trick her husband into joining The Club after his persistent refusal to accept the high honour, as most men would esteem it, of an invitation to join. Grote said that he 'always preferred dining at home to any other way of passing his evening'. There were others like him, in this respect. He lived to change his mind about The Club.

Sir Charles Dilke's biographers, Stephen Gwynn and Gertrude Tuckwell, tell in *The Life of the Rt. Hon. Sir Charles Dilke Bart., M.P.* (Vol. II, p. 25) how: 'Sir Charles Dilke was never a clubman and had incurred the remonstrances of Sir M. Grant Duff by refusing to take up membership of the Athenaeum, adding, under some obvious misapprehension, 'as he was entitled to do on entering the Cabinet.' There is, of course, no such open invitation to all Cabinet Ministers. They continued, 'But there is a Club more august than the Athenaeum, and here also Dilke showed indisposition to enter.' Dilke's own statement was: 'I had been much pressed to accept my election at Grillion's Club on Lord Salisbury's nomination. The Club considers itself such an illustrious body that it elects candidates without telling them they are proposed, and I received my notice accompanied by some congratulations. I at first refused to join, but afterwards wrote to the Secretary "Carlingford has been to see me about Grillion's, and tells me that I should have the terrible distinction of being the first man who ever declined to belong to it, an oddity which I cannot face so I will ask your leave to withdraw my refusal."' On May 3rd (1884) he wrote, 'I breakfasted at the Club for the first time, Mr. Gladstone and a good many other Front Bench people, chiefly conservative, being present.' This experience evidently converted him because later 'he spoke often of Grillion's, which he habitually frequented and much enjoyed'. Other distinguished men, as this book shows, also found membership of a good Club to be more rewarding than they had anticipated.

'Subscription Houses'

Already by the first quarter of the nineteenth century Clubs had become an established element in London social life. Their origin can be traced to the earlier coffee-houses and not to famous dining-clubs, meeting periodically in a private room of a tavern or hotel, which was the practice of the Society of Dilettanti, The Club and Grillion's Club, to mention the more renowned. Two splendid Clubhouses existed in St. James's Street, of which White's was the older (1755), Brooks's having moved there in 1778. White's Club had its origins much earlier in the coffee-house Mr. White opened in 1693. It was maintained after his death in 1711 by his widow and then after about 1730 by their former assistant, John Arthur. It was burnt down in 1733 and rebuilt. The first records of 'the Old Club' at White's date from 1736. Among its distinguished Members in the eighteenth century were Sir Robert Walpole, Lord Chesterfield, Edward Gibbon, Edmund Burke, Lord Anson, Lord Clive, Charles James Fox, George Selwyn, Horace Walpole and John Wilson Croker. Both White's and Brooks's were social-clubs, both renowned for the reckless, heavy gambling among some of their Members. They were also exclusive and small. White's was a Tory stronghold, Brooks's was Whig. According to Captain Gronow, in 1814–15 members of the only West End Clubs, White's, Boodles, Brooks's, Wattier's, the Guards', Arthur's and Graham's, 'almost without exception belonged exclusively to the aristocratic world . . . nearly all the noble families of Great Britain belonged to White's'. Many men who could not expect to be admitted to such preserves of privilege sought other, less fashionable Clubs where they would not be expected to stake their possessions on success at cards or with the dice or over some trivial bet.

Immediately after the victorious end of the long-drawn-out Napoleonic wars, the Travellers' Club was built in 1814 at the suggestion of Castlereagh. The United Service Club followed in 1815, to cater for Army Officers not below the rank of Major, and Captains and senior officers of Flag rank of the Royal Navy. A yet more impressively grand building, designed by Sir Robert Smirke, was erected on the west side of Trafalgar Square for the Union Club in 1822, which has been occupied since 1924 by offices of the Canadian Government in London. All were social-clubs to which the aristocracy, gentry, army and naval officers, political and administrative men could resort.

Who first thought that London society needed another Club such as the Athenaeum; who took the initiative to bring men together to create it; who those men were, and how they set about the task, are all questions likely to stimulate curiosity beyond the actual membership of the Club today, because they are questions about the social life and outlook of England during the first quarter of the nineteenth century. What can be discovered from correspondence and the first formal records of the foundation of the Athenaeum has been told in the careful record largely prepared by Henry Richard Tedder who served the Club for over forty years, first as Assistant Librarian and later as Secretary and Librarian from 1889 to 1924. His task was both prolonged and facilitated by the full set of Minute Books preserved among the Club's records. He died before he could complete the work, which was finished by Mr. Humphry Ward under the title *History of the Athenaeum 1824–1925*, 'Printed for the Club' in 1926. Its first 111 pages summarised some of the main developments to be found in the records of one hundred years of the Club's existence. In the remaining 240 pages brief biographical notes were given about all the men considered by the Club Committee to be sufficiently eminent to be invited (under the Club's Rule II) to join without going through the normal procedure of waiting for election after being proposed, seconded and supported by Members. It was a roll of honour of which any institution might be proud, because without exception, those so invited to join very readily did so. Well illustrated by photographs of the Club, of some of its rooms and with portraits of some eminent Members, Ward's was an impressive record worthy of the Club and the occasion; fitting evidence that membership of the Athenaeum had been well able to inspire that sentiment of respect, loyalty and affection that the Ancient Romans called *pietas*.

Ward's *History* has long been out of print. Since it was written changes more profound have occurred in Club and social life than those that happened within the century it commemorates. His book was a product of the Edwardian, if not essentially of the Victorian era; all the more valuable therefore because it preserves a flavour of those times. They now seem so distant that even many alive today with memories of their childhood before 1914, or before 1924, can be as astonished as any teenager by photographs of street scenes in London of that time which they themselves may have witnessed. Far more than buildings, clothes, transport and shops have been replaced by completely new models; the spirit of society is very different.

Anyone undertaking a sketch of a West End Club from its beginning until today becomes very conscious of the difficulty of indicating adequately how that spirit has changed, while at the same time showing how there has been a continuity of Club life with a vigorous resolution to maintain the values by which it was inspired and which it has fostered throughout a century and a half. The story of a Club such as the Athenaeum should not fail to interest anyone curious about the history of British social and cultural life. Others, whether as Members of the Club or of other Clubs, may like to know a little more about its remote and recent past. Those thinking of joining a Club or wondering perhaps what membership of a Club might add to their experience and their way of life, may derive some ideas on the subject from an indication of what the Athenaeum has stood for during its long, honourable and distinguished history.

Foundation and Early Years of the Athenaeum

The first notable fact about the history of the Athenaeum is the evidence its foundation brings of the extent to which British cultural life had developed since the days when a few choice spirits met at the Mitre Tavern.

John Wilson Croker (1780–1857), of Anglo-Irish parentage, is commonly regarded as the man who first had the idea that 'literary men and artists required a place of rendezvous'. Until the beginning of the nineteenth century it seems unlikely that there were sufficient men of literary and artistic distinction in London to make up a very considerable Club for them alone. Coffee-houses and taverns sufficed for the small groups that foregathered regularly. By 1823, however, Croker said that 'the University Club, the Travellers', the United Service and other Clubs had superseded and destroyed the old coffee-houses'. He did not mention the Alfred Club that had been founded in 1808 for men of letters, presumably so-called after that early King who strove to civilise his backward people. In that task it did not prove to be very successful. One Member was reported (by John Timbs in his *Clubs and Club Life in London*, 1872) as saying that it was 'the dullest place in the world where bores prevailed to the exclusion of every other interest, and one heard nothing but idle reports and twaddling opinions. It is the asylum of doting Tories and drivelling quidnuncs.' If this was true, it was not kind of Sir William Fraser to call it 'a sort of minor Athenaeum', which might account for the suggestion that the title should be changed from Alfred to 'Halfread'. It survived, however moribund, down to 1855, when it was amalgamated with the Oriental Club, a migration which is not recorded as amending the ancient wisdom to *ad orientem lux*.

Theodore Hook's frivolous jingle about Clubs began with

If a man loves comfort and has little cash to buy it, he
Should get into a crowded Club – a most select society

while the last quatrain mentioned the Alfred Club

For country squires the only Club in London now is
Boodle's, sirs,
The Crockford Club for playful men, the Alfred Club for
noodles, sirs.

Croker was thoroughly familiar with the fashionable Clubs of London as a Member of White's and the Union Club as well as Crockford's long before it became according to Gronow, 'a cheap dining house for Irish buckeens,[1] spring captains and "welchers" from Newmarket'. Croker must, therefore, have had a clear idea of what additional resources London would be likely to use at the time. He also had no doubt that they could be easily provided. 'All that is necessary to create a Club in these times is a Circular Letter of invitation', he said on 23 November 1823.

Croker had been prominent in promoting the Union Club, the plans for which he had printed on the Admiralty Press, presumably on repayment. He had

[1] 'A young man belonging to the "second rate" gentry of Ireland. A younger son of the poorer aristocracy having no profession and aping the manners of the wealthier classes.' *O.E.D.*

then for many years combined the duties of Secretary of the Admiralty with brilliant service as a Member of Parliament to the Tories whom he is supposed to have rechristened 'Conservatives'. He had helped Canning to found the *Quarterly Review* (1809) to which he became a prominent contributor, mainly of literary articles, now remembered only because one of them was a savage onslaught on *Endymion* (1818) which has been thought to have contributed to the decline of Keats. His biographer L. J. Jennings admitted that his opinions were sometimes prejudiced and one-sided, for he was a party-man of the old type. He had also serious faults of temper and manner, often 'overbearing and harsh, impatient of contradiction and somewhat given to self-assertion'.

Gronow, after an encounter with him at a dinner party in 1815, recorded: 'Croker was also agreeable, notwithstanding his bitter and sarcastic remarks upon everything and everybody. The sneering, ill-natured expression on his face struck me as an impressive contrast to the frank, benevolent countenance of Walter Scott.' In this vein Gronow once referred to Castlereagh as a 'splendid summit of bright and polished frost'. Yet it was also said of Croker that 'he had done a thousand kindly acts'. He certainly did not spare himself in his public duties or in his activities on behalf of the Athenaeum.

He sought support for his proposal first from Sir Humphry Davy, then President of the Royal Society, and, with his agreement, from 'each member of the Council of the Royal Society and each Royal Academician, with perhaps a dozen persons of acknowledged literary eminence such as Sir Walter Scott, Mr. Moore, Mr. Campbell, Mr. Rogers, Mr. Rose etc.' 'Our first rule', he said to Sir Humphry Davy, 'must be that no one shall be eligible except Gentlemen who have either published some literary or professional work or a paper in the Philosophical Transactions' (i.e. of the Royal Society). Bishops and judges, he thought, might be admitted, whether they had published anything or not. Sir Humphry Davy agreed, also suggesting 'Members of both Houses, none of whom can perform their high duties without a competent knowledge of literature'. Croker, who was one of them, may have agreed with John Cam Hobhouse whose experience of his fellow M.P.s led him to describe them as 'selfish, silly and unreasonable men', because no general admission of Members of Parliament, as such, without additional qualifications, occurred.

As a result of Croker's energetic preparations a distinguished Committee was formed, fourteen of whom, without Croker, met at the Royal Society where Sir Humphry Davy took the Chair on 16 February 1824 and 'Resolved. That the . . . Club is established this day'. They then named the first list of noblemen and gentlemen to be 'admitted into the Club'. They included William Blake,

F.R.S., Henry Hallam, John Herschell, the Rt. Hon. Robert Peel, George Rose and Lord John Russell. The task of completing the list, finding and furnishing premises and getting the Club into being was delegated to a working Sub-Committee consisting of the Earl of Aberdeen, Francis Chantrey, John Wilson Croker, Sir Humphry Davy, Davies Gilbert, Charles Hatchett, Richard Heber, Joseph Jekyll, Sir Thomas Lawrence, Edward Hawke Locker, the Rt. Hon. Sir Charles Long and Robert Smirke, Jr. Throughout 1824, but rarely with a full attendance, the Sub-Committee and the General Committee worked energetically at their task. By 22 May 1824 they were able to meet in the new house of the Club, No. 12 Waterloo Place, where the Union Club had begun. Before that date they had met at 22 New Street, Spring Gardens, the residence of Joseph Jekyll, a lawyer and Master in Chancery who took a leading part in the restoration of the Temple Church and Inn. 'Unfortunately few of his witticisms outlived him', said Humphry Ward, but his distinguished daughter Gertrude did, to take a lead in garden art in England.

On 1 March 1824 it was 'Resolved. That persons eligible to the Club shall be individuals known for their scientific or literary attainments, Artists of eminence in any of the Fine Arts and Noblemen and Gentlemen distinguished as liberal patrons of Science, Literature or the Arts.' Among the names then added to be invited to join were Thomas Campbell, Rev. T. R. Malthus, Rev. H. H. Milman, Francis Palgrave and the Duke of Wellington. On 8 March 1824 it was 'Resolved. That the name of the Club be *The Society*'. The Minute Book records on that date that 'Lord Althorp, Samuel Rogers, J. W. F. Herschell decline belonging to the Club' but they all soon changed their minds. Meetings of the Sub-Committee and General Committee continued weekly or fortnightly throughout 1824, except during August, principally to add new Members and to supervise the business affairs of the rented premises. Already by the 17th of May of that year the first list of Members was sent to be printed. On that day, in Croker's absence, the Sub-Committee considered that 'the title of *The Athenaeum* is preferable to that of *The Society*' and they arranged to have the change approved by the General Committee.

It was generally supposed that Croker was responsible for the change of name as he had been for founding the Club. In a letter to the *New Statesman* of 13 December 1952 it was alleged that Croker had proposed to Sir Humphry Davy, Sir Thomas Lawrence and others, described, without adequate evidence, as 'all notorious practical jokers', that the name should be the 'old English *Athelu-neum*, "noble family of corpses" ' to describe 'this congregation of noble but somewhat weighty and inert gentlemen'. Croker was credited as a young man, with a lively wit, but there is no record of his 'practical jokes'. The story itself seems a joke. The Members had not all been assembled when the name was chosen. It is unlikely that anyone would wish to create a club for corpses, however noble. If it was a joke, it lacked point because 'neum' is not an Anglo-Saxon word. Although the story was supported by the remark that Croker was 'something of a linguist', his abilities in that direction did not extend beyond Greek, Latin and French. As a classical scholar at Trinity College, Dublin, in 1796, he is unlikely to have had time to pursue Anglo-Saxon or Middle English even if courses in those languages had then been provided there. There is no evidence that he had any knowledge of either. On the other hand *Athenaeus*, 'of the City of Athens', would readily occur to anyone remembering Hadrian's Athenaeum or familiar with Lucretius or Livy. Later Croker was to give more practical testimony to his enthusiasm for things Greek.

As a beginning Club premises were hired at No. 12 Waterloo Place for £900 a year. A staff of seven men, three boys and five women servants was engaged at a cost of £551 a year; rent, coal and light cost £2,201; plate, linen, glass and furniture were chosen by Croker at a cost of £2,000. It was possible then to establish a Club for 500 Members at a cost of under £5,000. Michael Faraday (1791–1867), once a bookseller's apprentice, already rising to fame as Sir Humphry Davy's assistant, acted as Secretary for a few months. When he resigned in May 1824, because of his scientific work, he became a Member of the Club.

In June 1824 the first printed list of members contained 506 names including the King of the Belgians, H.R.H. the Duke of Sussex, Canning, Wellington, Peel, Russell, Aberdeen, Goderich and Palmerston. It represented, said Humphry Ward in 1926, 'every phase of the highest national intellectual character of the day and thus laid the foundation of what has been the chief characteristic of the Athenaeum during its hundred years of existence'. If any humble Member now repeated such a verdict, it might savour of the technique of indirect self-adulation.

What can and should be said is that it was not, like some of the older Clubs, a preserve of the aristocracy or of wealth. It was not that mythical entity, an 'exclusive élite', but, like all true élites, it was an 'inclusive élite' to which achievement in any eminent cultural activity qualified for admission. It is a distinction needing emphasis now that demagogic claptrap seeks to make 'élite' a 'smear-word' in relation to excellence in education, culture and manners, although not in the world of sport or entertainment. There, those whom demagogues seek to delude are quick to recognise and honour talent. Faraday who, because of his lowly social origin, was said to have been treated at first as a menial by Lady Davy, was an honoured Member, as was Sir Francis Chantrey, a Sheffield carpenter's son. Writing to his sister Hannah in 1831, Macaulay told her that 'when Chantrey dined with Rogers some time ago he took particular notice of the vase and the table on which it stands and asked Rogers who made the table. "A common carpenter," said Rogers. "Do you remember the making of it?" said Chantrey. "Certainly," said Rogers with some surprise. "I was in the room while it was finished with the chisel and gave the workman directions about placing it." "Yes," said Chantrey, "I was the carpenter. I remember the room well and all the circumstances." ' Macaulay commented that it was 'a curious story, I think, and honourable both to the talent which raised Chantrey, and to the magnanimity which kept him from being ashamed of what he had been.' Those were the days before the term 'working classes' had entered common usage and before Karl Marx had invented 'the proletariat'. Chantrey's was no solitary example. The father of Daniel Maclise, R.A., was a private in a Highland Regiment. John Gould, F.R.S., was the son of a gardener at Windsor Castle, Richard Cobden had been a clerk and commercial traveller, the father of W. P. Frith, R.A., was a butler. They were by no means the only distinguished Members of the Club to contradict the notion that economic or social 'class' distinctions were all-important in Victorian England. Faraday and Chantrey were Founder Members of the Club along with Samuel Rogers (1763–1855), a rich retired banker who winced when Sydney Smith referred to Rogers and Co. Many with similarly lowly social origins, have not merely been admitted but were invited by the Club's Committee to join, a mark of distinction still to be coveted. Naturally, the size of the accommodation available imposed a limit on the number of Members.

Sir Thomas Lawrence, R.A., who had earned a living at Bath with his pencil since the age of twelve, offered to provide the Club with a seal of its own. He drew the head of Athena which was executed by Chantrey and engraved by William Wyon (1795–1851), chief engraver at the Royal Mint. It is still used and the original is preserved among the heirlooms of the Club.

In November 1824 the Committee arranged for a conversazione to be held every Monday at 9 p.m. as a way of enabling Members to meet each other socially. Tea was provided from the Club funds from December onwards and a year later it was decided that 'each Member of the Committee attending the Monday evening meeting shall have the privilege of introducing one visitor'. There was no mention of ladies as possible guests.

In their first printed Report of 9 May 1825 the Committee referred to the 'satisfactory and prosperous state of the Institution' and their high hopes that it would be possible to find a suitable site and to build a Clubhouse. Already there was a waiting-list of hundreds of candidates for admission. At this time the Government decided to pull down the derelict Carlton House, the former home of George IV when Prince Regent, with its long frontage on Pall Mall and large garden behind, and to allow 'well-considered Clubs and private houses on the site' (a limitation disregarded by the Crown Estate Commissioners in recent years). It was then that Waterloo Place was extended to give access down Duke of York's Steps to the Mall. Negotiations were begun with the Commissioners of H.M. Woods, Forests and Land Revenues both by the United Service Club and the Athenaeum with the result that their Clubhouses now stand on the East and West side of the new Waterloo Place.

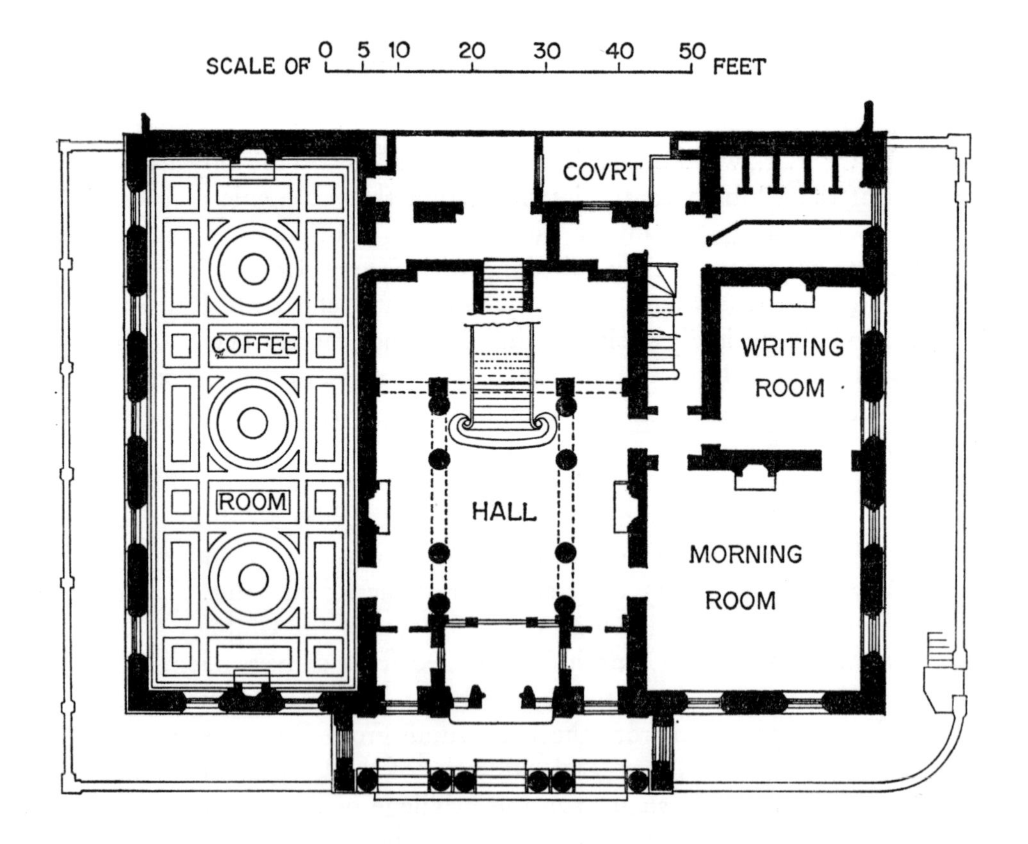

GROUND-FLOOR PLAN

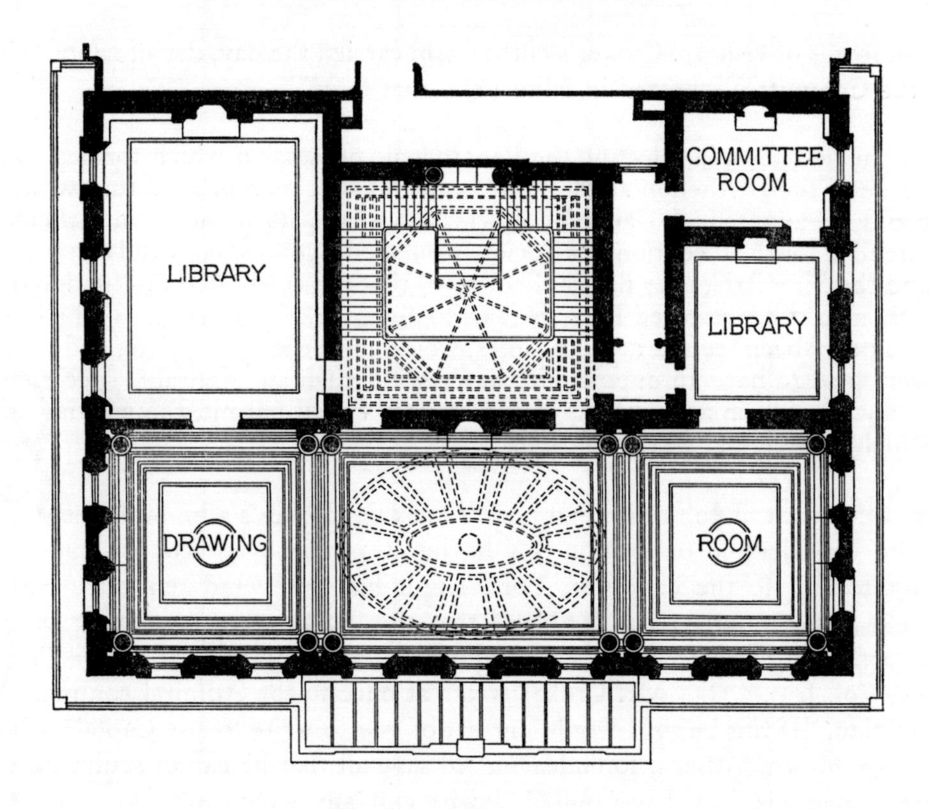

FIRST-FLOOR PLAN

Already by April 1824 the Club Committee had resolved that 'Decimus Burton Esq. be placed on the Committee and Sub-Committee' as the Club's architect. He was then only twenty-four years old, fresh from designing the archways at Hyde Park Corner in the neo-Greek style that had succeeded Robert Adam's novelties. By 1827 the site had been secured and by May 1828 the Committee reported that 'the building was proceeding with all possible speed'. Burton kept his promise to complete it by 1830 and in May of that year the Committee held its first meeting in the new building.

Croker's strong Classical interests are evident in the general design of the building and particularly in its external adornment by the statue of Athena over the entrance and the frieze round the top of the house. He, in common with Sir Thomas Lawrence and many others, had been profoundly stirred by Lord Elgin's rescue from demolition for building materials of some of the remaining fragments of the Parthenon at Athens. Deposited in the British Museum, they drew crowds of visitors. Croker's enthusiasm carried the day, despite opposition, for the Committee reported in May 1829 that they

> had no hesitation in selecting the Panathenaic procession which formed the frieze of the Parthenon as the most beautiful specimen of sculpture which could be adopted. To an edifice which borrows its name from Athens, intended for the reception of a Society professedly connected with Literature and the Fine Arts, they flatter themselves that the celebrated production of Athenian taste, restored here, as it is, to a degree of perfection in which it had never been seen in modern times, would not be inappropriate, and they were glad to have an opportunity of showing such an admirable specimen of ancient art, in as nearly as circumstances would permit, the position in which the original was employed.

It was the work of John Henning (1771–1851). Croker's admirable insistence, despite considerable opposition, on having this frieze reflects his energy in trying to add to the collection Lord Elgin had recovered ten years earlier. 'In 1822 reports arrived in England that the Turks were destroying part of the Parthenon,' wrote Croker's biographer (L. J. Jennings, *The Croker Papers*, 1885, Vol. I, p. 275), 'Mr. Croker wrote at once to the Admiral commanding the station, "If this be so, I would entreat of you to write to any Captain who is likely to go near Athens, to endeavour to save all that he can of sculpture that these barbarians may have pulled down; and any expense he may be at in purchasing or moving the fragments I shall most cheerfully pay, and he may draw on me for the amount." ' Over fifty years before 'Cleopatra's Needle' was brought to London in 1877, Croker had tried to get it, proposing to have it floated to London on a stout timber raft.

For all his hard work, good ideas and devotion to the truth as he saw it, Croker had been unfortunate in stirring up many enemies. They were not all his political opponents, among whom party spirit then took on a degree of rancour and hatred hardly equalled in our own time. John Cam Hobhouse, Lord Broughton, who listened to him in the House of Commons, thought him 'smart and insolent'. Croker's friends thought that he had trounced Macaulay in the climax to the great debate on the first Reform Bill of 1831, but the opposition were in no doubt that Macaulay had the best of it. Some of his political colleagues, notably Disraeli, gave more lasting and bitter expression to their dislike, for Croker was supposed to have been the model for the base and despicable Rigby in Disraeli's novel *Coningsby* (1844). More intense than the 'imperfect sympathies' to which Charles Lamb alluded, such virulence in public and private life is but one more testimony to the depressing conclusion *homo homini lupus*. Long after his death which occurred suddenly in 1857 at the age of seventy-seven, the Athenaeum was able to buy a splendid marble head of Croker, carved by Sir Francis Chantrey, R.A., for only twenty guineas, about one-tenth of what Chantrey would have charged.

Henry Crabb Robinson (1775–1867) who was among the earliest members, considered that he had done the Club a good service in opposing one of Croker's plans. Reminiscing in 1852 he recalled,

> The Right Honourable Wilson Croker . . . according to common report was the officious manager and despot, ruling the Club at his will. . . . The Committee had meant to have a neat portico of four columns – the one actually erected – but Croker had arbitrarily changed the plans and the foundations were then digging for a portico of two columns, not at all becoming so broad a space as the front comprises.

Robinson raised the matter at the General Meeting, and, despite Croker's opposition, carried the original plan for which he was thanked by the architect. His thanks will be echoed by all who know the story (not mentioned in Ward's *History*). There are, in fact, six columns, the middle columns being adjacent pairs.

Description of the Athenaeum's Clubhouse, 1830–1900

Towards the end of the nineteenth century fifty copies of a small pamphlet by the Rev. Francis Gledstanes Waugh, M.A. (Oxon.), 'The Athenaeum Club and its Associations' were printed by the author 'for Private Circulation'. In addition to quoting amusing anecdotes about some members, Waugh gave a description of the Club. Its external measurements were 104 ft by 78 ft. Croker, he said, had watched every detail of its construction.

> Worried as the architect was by Mr. Croker, it is probable that Mr. Croker was worried still more by his own friends. One subject in particular occasioned much controversy. Many members were anxious to have what at that time was considered an important adjunct to a mansion – an ice-house. This did not commend itself to the more aesthetic mind of the Secretary of the Admiralty, who was determined that John Henning, the Scotch artist, should sculpture for them a frieze, copied from that of the Parthenon. The opposition to this 'extravagant novelty' did not subside when the chairman reported that the frieze and cornice (which they had *already* ordered) would cost £2165. 1s. 10d. Croker, as usual, ultimately had his own way, thereby giving rise to the epigram –

I'm John Wilson Croker,
I do as I please;
Instead of an Ice-house,
I give you – a *Frieze*.

The structure exhibits beautiful lines, the parts are excellently proportioned, and for chasteness and purity of design it is probably unrivalled. The portico has a stately air. The balcony is extremely light and elegant; and with the classical tripod-flambeaux at its angles, is interesting as a specimen of iron-work treated on *Grecian* principles. The piercing of the casements and their relation to the wall-space is very striking. On a winter's night, when the building is lighted up from top to bottom, the effect is imposing and palatial, and the tall windows are revealed in all their grace. The area is surrounded by a parapet-wall marked out into compartments and decorated with slabs of green marble, and the whole is finished with a balustrade running round the roof.

From Waterloo Place some half-a-dozen marble steps lead into the Roman–Doric entrance portico, supported by six fluted columns, and having a frieze ornamented with triglyphs.[1] It was once when descending this flight that –

The poet of Hope,
Brimful of good liquor, as gay as the Pope,

lost his equilibrium, and thereby gave occasion to the convivial companion arm-in-arm with him to remark – 'Not

"Iser rolling rapidly,"[2]

but *we*, Sir!' The portico is surmounted by Baily's majestic statue of Athena, represented holding out her prone hand as if welcoming worshippers into her temple. The somewhat unprotected situation of the goddess has given rise to the following lines –

All ye who pass by, just stop and behold,
And say – Don't you think it a sin
That Minerva herself is left out in the cold,
While her *owls* are all gorging within?

1 It will be remembered that Maclise's portrait of Theodore Hook includes a sketch of the entrance to this his favourite haunt.

2 Since the days of Lamb and Hood such puns as a form of humour have become as outmoded as Campbell's 'Pleasures of Hope' may be thought to be.

Pushing open two pairs of folding-doors (having, in the vestibule between, the porter's lobby to the left, and a small waiting-room to the right), we enter the hall. This has always been justly admired, and a considerable amount of accommodation has been sacrificed to it. It is finely proportioned, being 59 ft long, 35 ft broad, and 21 ft high – or 54 ft at the highest; and underwent in 1891 an elaborate redecoration, Graeco-Roman in character, under the personal superintendence of E. J. Poynter, R.A., Director of the National Gallery, L. Alma-Tadema, R.A., and Arthur Lucas. [When it became necessary to repaint the hall and grand staircase in 1904 Sir Lawrence Alma-Tadema's colour and decorations were copied, but they have not survived.] Eight ivory-white pillars, with gilded capitals copied from the Choragic Monument of Lysicrates, support the wagon roof, which is adorned with compositions after the designs of L. Alma-Tadema. The walls are painted in primrose yellow of various tints. The front door is dadoed with pavonazetto and other coloured marbles, the back with green cipolino, while part of the staircase is panelled with fine slabs of breccia. The floor is Roman mosaic. The pendent electroliers are peculiarly classical.

Here, again, the Greek spirit will be noted in the fireplaces on either side, and the niches above them, which are occupied by statues (the 'Venus Victrix' and the 'Diana Robing') chosen by Sir Thomas Lawrence, P.R.A.

To the right of the hall is the newspaper or morning room, 30 ft by 30 ft, and 21 ft high, with two windows looking into Waterloo Place, and two into Pall Mall. This was redecorated in the autumn of 1892. The ceiling was adorned with designs in blue and gold by E. J. Poynter, R.A., after an old Venetian pattern, while in this, as in the other apartments on the ground floor, the original windows were replaced with plate-glass in polished mahogany frames.

On the left of the hall is the dining-room, 75 ft by 30 ft by 25 ft, having five windows fronting the garden, and two facing Waterloo Place. It was redecorated in 1892, and its ceiling and walls richly ornamented after Pompeian designs by E. J. Poynter, R.A. The panels were originally intended to receive pictures representing memorable incidents in the lives of distinguished members, but this design has never been carried out. Although the stranger is not admitted within its gates, he may, perhaps, be fortunate enough to be bidden to one of the 'Members' Dinners,' which are occasionally given in the room opposite.

The grand 'flying' staircase, which faces the entrance is of an unusual scale, considering the size of the building, and was greatly admired by Mr. Beckford, who pronounced it equal to anything of the kind he had seen abroad. It is lighted by an octagonal-domed lantern. The iron banisters and their treatment may be noticed with approval. Opposite us, and over the clock, is a gilded cast of the Apollo Belvedere, by George Rennie, while on the gallery are 'Eve at the Fountain', and the group of 'Poetry and Painting,' the work (and gift) of E. H. Baily, R.A. On the walls beneath are bassi-relievi of Thorwaldsen.

From the landing two doors lead into the drawing-room. This is one of the finest in London, being 100 ft long, 30 ft wide, and 27 ft high, and occupies the whole of the east side of the house. It was redecorated in 1893, aluminium being extensively used at the suggestion of L. Alma-Tadema, R.A. It is lighted by eleven windows, with French sashes, and twelve columns and sixteen pilasters support the ceiling. Here, too, we may commend the propriety of the details – the treatment of the fireplaces and marble mantelpieces, of the mirrors superimposed, and of the surrounding book-cases – all admirably proportioned. In an engraving made soon after its opening, it looks somewhat dreary and bare, although among the scant furniture were examples of the best kind of cabinet-work of the time; but now, with its abundance of fauteuils and sofas, it is essentially a cheerful apartment, and the chief resort for reading and conversation. Five o'clock finds it at the fullest, and at that hour daily during the season in no other chamber probably in Europe could such an assemblage of men of varied distinction be seen at once.

At the south-west end of the drawing-room a glazed door leads into the chief glory of the Athenaeum – its library. This is a lofty and comfortable apartment (43 ft long, 30 ft wide, and 23 ft high), and lighted by three windows, which overlook the garden. It is completely walled with books, access to the upper shelves being afforded by two light galleries. As illustrating its growth, we may note that on the club entering the present building it possessed nearly 4,000 volumes; in 1844 these had multiplied to 20,300; in 1852 the number was computed at about 31,000; in 1882 they amounted to 48,000; while in 1894 they approximated 61,000. So rapid and irrepressible has been the increase that it has overflowed the space originally allotted. Almost every place where shelves can be erected is occupied, and resort has often been had to the objectionable practice of putting volumes in a second row and packing them behind others. In 1889, however, a store was arranged upstairs with sufficient cases to provide for the overplus literature of some years to come.[1]

[1] It is computed that about 230 volumes and 70 pamphlets are annually added either by purchase or by donation, exclusive of the continuation of Works in Progress, of Transactions, Journals, and other Periodical Publications.

John Wilson Croker, Founder of the Club,
by Sir Francis Chantrey, R.A.

Decimus Burton, Architect of the Club House.

The Entrance Hall and Grand Staircase

CHAPTER TWO

The Club in Being

Nearly a century has elapsed since the Rev. Francis Waugh wrote the description of the Club quoted above, during which period there have been changes, notably in decoration and the disposition of some of the rooms. Rules have changed also. 'Strangers', first grudgingly allowed to dinner and later to lunch in a small room, are now admitted to the dining-room, or Coffee-Room as it is called (although coffee is no longer served there except at breakfast or at Speaker's dinners). Five o'clock in the afternoon no longer finds the Drawing-Room 'at the fullest', for Clubs are no longer as much frequented as formerly after lunch. Men no longer have the leisure that their predecessors seem to have enjoyed. Many do not live in London, but either come by train or drive to Town, which they leave as soon as they are able in the evening. It is at lunch-time rather than at tea-time that the Drawing-Room is fullest. According to Thomas Walker (*The Original*, 9 September 1835), 'the daily average of dinners was forty seven'. Afterwards, 'in those hours of the evening which are peculiarly dedicated to society . . . on an average twenty Members could not be counted.' Walker forecast habits then yet to come when he wrote (28 October 1835) in favour of 'a simple well-conceived dinner, instead of the luncheon now in vogue; then tea, with that excellent adjunct scarcely ever enjoyed in these days, buttered toast, about the present dinner hour, and a savoury little supper about half-past nine or ten, with a bowl of negus or some other grateful diluted potation after.' Such a change in habits had already occurred by 1911, when Ralph Nevill, speaking of the now defunct Marlborough Club, said 'At night like many other Clubs, it is now generally more or less empty.' Apart from such details, Waugh's description is still sufficiently accurate.

All that the Club's historian had to say in 1926 about Burton's achievement was that (in 1830) 'on the whole the Committee and the members at large were fairly well satisfied'. He then cautiously claimed that 'the success of Burton's work has been generally admitted for a hundred years'. In 1974 it is possible to be more generous and emphatic.

Since 1924, when the existence of a building such as that of the Athenaeum could be taken almost as a matter of course, several developments have thrown its outstanding quality into stronger relief. The immense damage sustained by the buildings of London during the aerial bombardment in the years of the Second World War of 1939–44 brought home to Londoners how fortunate they were not to have lost more. If the Athenaeum had not escaped with little worse than the loss of some windows, it seems unlikely that it could have been restored as it stands today. Architectural standards are not what they were. Under the pressure of cost-accounting provoked by the high cost of sites, materials and skilled labour, all architectural magnificence, even on the relatively small scale of the Athenaeum Clubhouse, seems to have been ruled out of consideration. It is a long time since any building of comparable architectural elegance has graced the streets of London. Where nineteenth-century Clubhouses have been demolished in order to profit from their vastly enhanced site-value, their replacement however 'functional', 'efficient', 'economical', 'contemporary', and so forth, has been at the expense of their former space, elegance, dignity, often magnificence, in construction, decoration and equipment. Many also feel that another valuable, less tangible quality has also been lost. It is not merely Clubhouses whose disappearance and replacement by cement, steel and glass constructions now causes lamentation, because many other buildings of character have suffered a like fate.

Not, of course, that this is a new experience in any city. Both the Athenaeum and the United Service Club rose on the ruins of Carlton House. Its loss and that of the neighbouring old Star and Garter Hotel where the Dilettanti used to meet, were deplored at the time, as by a friend of the Prince Regent, Captain Charles Morris (1745–1838):

> Again farewell! for ill my sight can bear
> Thy crumbling ruins, once so famed and fair.
> What art thou now? a heap of rubbish'd stone
> 'Pride, pomp and circumstance' for ever gone.

Carlton House had once belonged to Alexander Pope's friend, Richard Boyle, Earl of Burlington, from whom in 1732 it was acquired for Frederick Prince of Wales. In 1830 it was said to be in a ruinous condition. Gronow described it as 'one of the meanest and most ugly edifices that ever disfigured London . . . it was condemned by everybody who possessed taste'. Canova called it 'an ugly barn'. Its replacement by the United Service Club, Waterloo Place, and the Athenaeum, was not unworthy of the standards of the past but, in the circumstances, can be regarded as a contribution to the improvement in the appearance of the area, more particularly because it was but a part of the grand plan of Nash and the Prince Regent to cut an impressive new road, Regent Street, through sordid slums to the peace and beauty of the new Regent's Park. Today such a verdict can rarely be bestowed with any enthusiasm upon many of the utilitarian buildings, created, it would seem, by civil engineers rather than by architects, to house a maximum number of persons in a minimum amount of space. By such modern standards, surviving Georgian and Regency Clubhouses of London are extravagantly wasteful of space. They were built for men of taste who were fortunately less restricted by considerations of cost. Captain Morris, resenting the loss of 'the shady side of Pall Mall', lamented that

> Where thy Muse long ply'd her welcome toil
> Cold speculation barters out the soil.

A century and a half later his words bite home with much greater justice than they then could claim.

Improvements in the Nineteenth Century

With no lack of confidence, the Club Committee faced in 1830 the problem of paying for their splendid new Clubhouse. They had to raise £43,101. 14s. 8d. There was already a reserve fund, and at the first meeting in the new building plans were made to find an additional £20,000 needed to pay off the Club's debt. As later in the Club's history, any suggestion that the annual subscription should be raised encountered fierce opposition. Instead, an additional 200 Members were admitted. An Election Committee was appointed to recruit one hundred; another hundred were to be elected from the waiting-list in the normal way. Chantrey, R.A., Davies Gilbert, F.R.S., Adam Sedgwick, Croker, Thomas Moore, James Mill, the Marquess of Lansdowne and Henry Hallam formed the Election Committee. Among the men it chose were Macaulay, J. S. Mill and Thomas Barnes, editor of *The Times*. Macaulay had not then clashed with Croker in the debates over the first Reform Act, and his antipathy to the Club's founder had not yet developed.

Among those elected by the normal procedure was Charles Austin (1799–1874), friend of Macaulay and J. S. Mill, one of the wealthiest and most applauded lawyers of the day who, however, left little written work to testify to the ascendancy he exercised over his contemporaries. With the election of Sir Francis Goldsmid and Sir Charles Montefiore, the Athenaeum demonstrated the feelings that many of its Members entertained against the civil disabilities of the Jews that were not removed until 1859. More surprising in view of his chequered career, which had sent him to jail because of administrative irregularities in Mauritius, for which he had to take responsibility, was the election of Theodore Hook (1788–1841). He had been rescued and befriended by Croker and was, with Croker, a Member of the slightly older Union Club. His lively wit made him a centre of attraction, to the benefit of many Members and of the Club for he regularly dined there. He had also been a Founder Member of the Garrick Club in 1831 where he became 'the prime jester of the place . . . buoyant and irresistible, he was certainly the most original of all our wits', said Percy Fitzgerald in his *History of the Garrick Club* (1904, p. 21), where he also commended Hook's 'unmatched feat at the piano of extemporising verses on everyone present'.

Splendid as the Club's new building was, it had been equipped with gas fittings (at a cost of £772) which at that time were of the open-flare type emitting poisonous fumes and heat, unpleasant for human beings and destructive of the leather bindings in the Library. So rapid and severe was their decay that volumes which had hitherto survived unharmed for a century or more were visibly perishing. 'The cause is doubtful and remains under investigation', said the Club's Annual Report in 1839. Faraday and two binders went to work and by 1841 he had correctly traced the trouble to the open-gas flare-burners. He found remedy in the ventilation, the greater use of wax candles and a moister atmosphere. To secure such improvements he invented new apparatus that was installed at a cost of about £360. In 1844 the Committee reported their belief 'that the destructive process under which the books were suffering has been completely stopped'. They added that 'the difference of atmosphere is too obvious not to have been noticed'. Complaints continued, however, even after the installation of Faraday's 'Perfection Ventilation Apparatus', an improved gas-burner enclosed in glass which sent the fumes into the open air, by natural means, however, without forced-intake or extract. One Member, according to the Rev. F. G. Waugh, 'complained that gas produced "in combination with the breathings of seventy or eighty gastronomers, and the vapours arising from the dinners they are eating, an atmosphere wherein no animal ungifted with copper lungs, can long exist." '

Since gas was first installed in 1830, when £474 was spent on it and only £133. 18s. on lamp oil and wax, its use must have been reduced, as less was spent on it. In 1856, for example, £352 was spent on lamp oil and wax but only £200 on gas. By 1863 the situation was reversed. Gas then accounted for £505 while lamp oil cost £193 and wax candles £40. In 1857 'gas for kitchen stoves' first appears in the annual balance sheet. Further improvements were reported in gas equipment. One 'Sun burner' with sixty-three jets had been installed in the South Library in 1848 at a cost of £90 after successful trials with it in the Drawing-Room. Electricity derived from the Club's own generators was first used in 1886. They continued in operation until the St. James's and Pall Mall Electricity Company undertook the supply ten years later. In 1855 the first payment occurs (of £31. 10s.) in the Club's accounts for the 'Electric Telegraph despatches'.

In 1838 the heavy expense caused by renovations and the effort to improve the ventilation of the Club again found the Members unwilling to pay an increased annual subscription. Instead, forty new Members were elected. They were, said Darwin in his *Autobiography*, called 'the forty thieves'. He was one of them, along with Charles Dickens, Richard Monckton-Milnes, George Grote, Arthur Stanley, George Cattermole, J. D. Harding, Sydney Smirke, Philip Hardwick, Macready and others. Two years later the Club's 1830 debt of £20,000 had been reduced to £6,000.

Inevitably the history of a building can do no more than record such minor events as its erection, equipment, restorations and improvements. Many such matters are common to other buildings in London and call for no special notice, although they have an antiquarian interest for Members of a Club and others curious about the first introduction of many of the conveniences of modern life.

When it was decided to install Faraday's improved gas lighting and to effect other renovations the Club had to be closed for three months. Arrangements to exchange hospitality on such occasions with other Clubs were dismissed unanimously by the Committee as 'not conducive to the best interests of the Athenaeum'. This stand-off attitude persisted until 1863 when an agreement was reached with the United Universities Club and then in 1865 with the United Service Club, a pleasantly friendly compact that fortunately has already passed its centenary. In 1845, during alterations and improvements to the building, three rooms were rented for the Club in the British Coffee-House, or Hotel, in Cockspur Street.

Other physical improvements included the water supply. A well had been dug in 1830 from which the Club was supplied, with supplements as necessary from St. Martin's Pump (reserved for tea- and coffee-making) and the Chelsea Water Works. In 1855 the United Service Club found the water from Chelsea too dirty for baths. Ten years later its well water was also said to be unfit to drink. Eventually the Athenaeum was able to lay on a supply under public control enabling the Club's well to be filled in, but not until 1853, after the outbreak of cholera in London in 1849. Two years later the Club was connected to a main drainage system, although the first of London's two new main sewers was not completed until 1861.

Club histories, and other accounts of vanished ways, usually seem to regard what Victorian decorum dismissed as 'the usual domestic offices', as being beneath the dignity of history. Anyway, little is said about that necessary article of immemorial antiquity, the chamber-pot. Some old Club-men were able to recall memories of these 'articles', as elimination's artful aid, to astonish young recruits to London Clubs not so very long ago. At the United Service Club in 1820, two mahogany chamber-pot cupboards were ordered for the drawing-room, a similar provision already having been made for the dining-room at an early date. Forgotten today as insignificant in the grand pageantry of social history, such an obscure item in a Club's accounts needs to be remembered if ever great surprise is expressed that it was a long while before the possibility of admitting ladies to gentlemen's Clubs was even considered. A 'Self-acting water-closet' was demonstrated to the Club Committee in 1824 and such novelties were included, along with gas-lighting, when the Clubhouse was built, but not to the exclusion of chamber-pots. In 1829 Croker would have been able to see a water-closet in action at the Union Club, but rules about chamber-pots were still being made there in 1839. A serious defect of early water-closets was their lack of a trap to exclude offensive fumes from the cesspool or sewer to which they were connected. Burton's water-closet lavatories at the Athenaeum were said to have been 'up to the standard of his time', which may have seemed adequate then, although that 'standard' was supposed to have led to the death of the Prince Consort from typhoid at Windsor Castle in 1861. It was not until 1885 that the drainage system at the Athenaeum which, said Waugh, 'was found to be of a primitive description' was put in better order.

Heating in London's winter months was, of course, from open coal-fires, until 1869 when a 'new steam boiler' and radiators were installed at a cost of over £4,000. Since the end of the Second World War, except for smokeless solid fuel, open coal-fires have been banned in London, to the relief of struggling servants who had to carry supplies to all floors in the Athenaeum, and to the immense improvement of London's atmosphere until a new form of poison, the more deadly because invisible, from the exhaust of oil and petrol internal-combustion motor engines, annulled much of the benefits. In the Athenaeum several gas-fires and two fireplaces for smokeless fuel now supplement the Club's oil-fired central heating. Londoners today need an explanation of the phrase

Macaulay heard outside the Athenaeum, 'the blacks are flying'. It was increasingly repeated after his day because the rain of black specks of soot to which it referred was a constant and steadily increasing plague.

In 1900 an earlier hydraulic lift was replaced by a commodious electrically operated lift or elevator, installed to reduce the amount of stair-climbing which must have made the Drawing-Room and Library out of bounds to Members with weak hearts in earlier years. Very rarely the lift was liable to raise rather than stabilise blood pressure. Mr. M. T. Tudsbery recalls the extremity to which an elderly Member was reduced when returning late one Saturday night to seek his bedroom on the top floor with the aid of the lift. He had the misfortune to get trapped because the lift stopped between two floors. His shouts of mingled rage and frustration at length brought the night-porter who surveyed the scene in considerable perplexity before he announced to the enraged victim in slow, calm, deliberate tones, 'I'm very sorry, Sir, but there is nothing we can do about it until Monday morning'.

Not until the middle of the century was any attempt made to provide accommodation for smokers, due to the fierce opposition in all Clubs to tobacco smoking in any form. Towards the end of the eighteenth century it was a declining habit. In 1773 Samuel Johnson said that it 'had quite gone out'. The gentry bought snuff instead from the still extant 'Old Snuff House' in the Haymarket from 1720 onwards. Spanish snuff, favoured by the Prince Regent, cost £3 a pound. According to the historian of White's, snuff was more popular than pipes or cigars up till about 1859. Cigars and pipes were long held at bay. Repeated efforts, which the Prince of Wales was known to support strongly, to allow smoking at White's were renewed after he had joined the Club in 1856. They were defeated. As a result, the Prince aided the foundation of the Marlborough Club and rarely went inside White's. (According to the historian of White's the failure of the Prince to secure the election there of a rich Jewish moneylender from whom he had borrowed heavily was the real cause of his aversion.) Queen Victoria so strongly disapproved of the habit that when Palmerston was a guest at Windsor Castle he smoked his cigars in the fire-place of his room.

Two snuff-boxes were ordered for the Athenaeum in 1825. During the nineteenth century the Club spent anything up to £20 (gold) a year on snuff. In recent times there have been complaints when the solitary silver-mounted snuff-horn in the Drawing-Room was found empty. Smokers in the Athenaeum won their first, although minor victory when, by one vote in a hotly contested division in 1862, they managed to gain one small room, barely sixteen feet square, at the top of the house, as 'the Smoking Room' into which no more than four or five smokers could crowd. Thackeray was often among them, and no doubt Carlyle also, who was recruited under Rule II in 1853. For years Members appealed in vain for better accommodation, so the battle continued. How backward the Athenaeum was in tolerating tobacco smoke was brought out by a survey of the amount of space available for smokers in sixteen other London Clubs, printed in the Committee's Annual Report in 1868. Then, at last, more space was grudgingly provided by taking over an underground room used as a Servants' Hall and enlarging it by excavating another room which also became the Billiards Room. These extensive operations required a new staircase, so the total cost between 1868 and 1869 was over £15,000 (gold).

It comes as a shock to read in the histories of the United Service Club, whose Members were all Senior Naval and Military Commanders, and of the Union Club, that complaints arose because some Members were in the habit of spitting on the carpets and elsewhere in their Clubs. This objectionable habit, sometimes attributed to the increasing use of tobacco, prompted the invention of spittoons, an article that remained in use in the United States for many years after it had disappeared from London. Smoking in the Drawing-Room of the Athenaeum was not permitted until 1924 and then only after 1.30 p.m. In 1928 the Club Committee extended the permission to all hours. Thirty members joined in a protest against this innovation which was then put to a vote. A majority of Members were still opposed but they fell short of the two-thirds needed, so the protest failed. Today only in the South Library and the Coffee-Room is smoking not allowed, often to the embarrassment of some Members who may entertain guests accustomed to the American habit of lighting a cigarette between courses at meals.

A bare narrative about Club buildings is of minor concern in comparison with the human interest in what went on inside. It seems that the enormity of the offence of smoking was such that Theodore Hook made no mention of it in a satirical piece he wrote on 'Clubs'. No Club was indicated as the scene of the rudeness and insolence he depicted, so there is no reason to suppose that he had the Athenaeum specially in mind. As an indication of the kind of behaviour that might be observed at that time, there is some interest still in his paragraphs which aimed at giving recently admitted candidates a few leading rules for their behaviour, in the way of directions – thus:

> In the first place find fault with everything and bully the waiters. What do you pay your subscriptions for, but to secure that privilege? Abuse the

Committee for mismanagement, until you get on it yourself – then abuse everybody else.
Never shut the door of any room into which you may go, or out of which you may come.
When the evening papers arrive, pounce upon three; keep one in your hand reading, another under your arm, ready to relieve that and sit down upon the third. By this means you possess yourself of the opinions of all parties, without being influenced by anyone else.
If you wish to dine early and cheap, order some cold meat just before three o'clock; it will then be charged as luncheon – bread, pickles, etc. gratis. Drink table beer, because, as the Scotch gentleman said of something very different, 'it is very pleasant, and it costs nothing.'
If you dine on the joint, get it first and cut all the best parts of it and help yourself to twice as much as you want, for fear that you should never see it again. If you are inclined to read the newspaper when you have finished your meat, make use of the cheese as a reading desk; it is very convenient, and, moreover, makes the paper smell of cheese and the cheese taste of the paper.
If you come in and see a man whom you know, dining quietly by himself, or two men dining sociably together, draw up your chair to their table and volunteer to join them. This they cannot very well refuse, although they may wish you at old Scratch. Then call for the bill of fare and order your dinner, which, as the two others had half done before your arrival, will not be served till they have quite finished theirs. This will enable them to enjoy the gratification of seeing you proceed through the whole of your meal, from soup to cheese inclusive while they are eating their fruit and sipping their wine. If you call for tea, call for a 'cup' of tea; when the waiter has brought it abuse him for its being too strong, and desire him to fetch an empty cup and a small jug of boiling water; then divide the tea into the two cups and fill up both with water. By this method, you get two cups of tea for the price of one. N.B. the milk and sugar not charged for.
If you are a literary man, always write your books at the Club – pen, ink and paper gratis; a circumstance which is likely to make your productions profitable.
When there is a ballot, blackball everybody you do not happen to know. If a candidate is not one of your particular acquaintances, he cannot be fit to come there . . .
Always walk about the coffee room with your hat on, to show your independence and your respect for the numerous noblemen and gentlemen who are sitting at dinner without theirs.
When you go away, if it is a wet night, and you are without a cloak or a great-coat, take the first that fits you, you can send it back in the morning, when it is fine; remember you do. This rule equally applies to umbrellas.

Few, if any Clubmen are likely now to recognise one of their fellow Members after reading this description, although many, even in the Athenaeum, may have cause for annoyance in the matter of evening papers, while umbrellas are stolen at some Clubs as Athenaeum Members may have had cause to realise when as visitors they have taken theirs with them. If Theodore Hook's satire is to be taken seriously, as a sample of the manners of the British in the early nineteenth century, there is reason to believe that some standards of behaviour have since improved; the world that his words revive has as little relevance to our own times as the granite blocks on the edge of the pavement on the east side of the Athenaeum, which were put there, as a small tablet records, to enable the Duke of Wellington to mount upon and alight from his horse more easily on his journeys to and from Apsley House to the Athenaeum.

It seems that the desire to smoke became more acute after Hook's day, gaining adherents steadily until, in recent years, an active campaign to discourage it on health grounds endeavoured gradually to arrest its advance. Smoking certainly seems less in evidence in recent years. Among other changes in social habits that some Members have noticed with relief is the rarity now of the sound of deep snoring that could formerly shatter the calm of the Drawing-Room.

Up to the turn of the century, the only major alterations in the Club building have been the addition of a new top storey in 1898 and its replacement by two storeys in 1927/8. Complaints had long been heard about the need for more accommodation. An effort to secure bedrooms for Members was made in 1874 when it was proposed to acquire corner premises in Pall Mall and Waterloo Place opposite the Club and to connect them with the Club by an underground passage. It was defeated because the cost would have been too great. In 1898 a recessed top storey, designed by T. E. Collcutt, was added to provide rooms for the Secretary, the Librarian, serving rooms and about ten small bedrooms for the women servants. Members benefited by the creation of the large Upper Smoking-Room (80 ft by 24 ft) running along the whole south side of the Club which was then called the Card-Room because of the number of Members who regularly spent some hours there every afternoon and evening playing whist, and later in the present century, bridge. It also housed nearly 8,000 books.

A growing demand for bedrooms for Club Members at last led to the setting up of a special Committee whose detailed study and plans for a new top storey were accepted in 1927 although they involved an increase of the annual subscription to £15. 15s. a year. Nearly all West End Clubs then required as much.

In order to effect the transformation the Club was closed from 29 August 1927 to 6 February 1928, Members being divided between six other Clubs as guests. Then also the opportunity was taken for other improvements in reforming the lavatory arrangements, entailing the disappearance of the last chamber-pots, extending the central heating, painting the exterior and redecorating the Drawing-Room and staircase. At a total cost of £28,847 which included £2,000 for furniture, the Club's accommodation was improved to look much as it does today. Members' bedrooms were then provided at the expense of the staff who had to be lodged elsewhere at a charge to the Club of about £800 a year. In addition to raising the subscription to fifteen guineas a year, the Club issued redeemable notes of £25 without interest. Members taking them up were allowed to deduct a guinea from their annual subscription for each note they acquired, up to a limit naturally of fifteen notes. It was a successful device. All notes were soon over-subscribed with a waiting-list ready to take over any that lapsed. By 1929 the whole cost of the improvements had been defrayed, and by the end of 1929 the Club had a surplus balance of £1,537.

Merely to be able to reprint, for each tenth year, a Club menu card and wine list at dinner, giving also the time at which meals were consumed, would interest many people today, but unfortunately such ephemeral facts were not preserved. It matters less because other menus and cookery books of nineteenth-century England sufficiently illustrate this aspect of the period.

Yet of far greater interest would be an account of what was said and what was written within the Athenaeum's hospitable walls, especially within the Library which demands a brief description along with an account of its cost and the Club finances in general. Something more will be said about such matters, but they would hardly possess much significance without some prior realisation of the force of the tangible attractions that assured a Club such as the Athenaeum of a place in the hearts of many eminent men and earned it, therefore, a niche in the history of British social and cultural life.

Members of the Athenaeum in the early days of the nineteenth century, a number of whom were also Members of the very limited private dining-clubs meeting occasionally, were no foes of conviviality. The Athenaeum, in common with other such Clubs, had however the enormous advantage over the dining-clubs of a large and elegant building to which Members could repair at almost any hour, Saturdays and Sundays included; where they were all respectfully recognised, and where they could feel thoroughly at home. There, they were not compelled to eat a beef steak or starve. In addition there was the immense advantage of the Library, growing greater and more useful every year, where books, newspapers and magazines, English and foreign, were readily available.

Some of the many merits of these new facilities provided by the permanent establishment of Clubs have often been described by those who, in their own individual manner, have been able to enjoy them throughout one hundred and fifty years. An early tribute to the newly erected Athenaeum Club was printed by Thomas Walker (1784–1836) in his periodical *The Original*, the first number of which appeared in May 1835.

> One of the most important changes in society is the present system of clubs. The facilities of living have been wonderfully increased by them in many ways, whilst the expense has been greatly diminished. For a few pounds a year, advantages are to be enjoyed which no fortune except the most ample can procure. I can best illustrate this by a particular instance. The only club I belong to is the 'Athenaeum', which consists of twelve hundred members, amongst whom are a large proportion of the most eminent persons in the land in every line, – civil, military, and ecclesiastical; peers, spiritual and temporal, commoners, men of the learned professions, those connected with science, the arts and commerce, in all its principal branches as well as the distinguished who do not belong to any particular class. Many of these are to be met with every day, living with the same freedom as in their own houses for twenty-five guineas entrance and six guineas a-year. Every member has the command of an excellent library, with maps; the daily papers, English and Foreign; the principal periodicals, and every material for writing, with attendance. The building is a sort of palace, and is kept with the same exactness and comfort as a private dwelling. Every member is a master, without any of the trouble of a master. He can come when he pleases, and stay away as long as he pleases, without anything going wrong. He has the command of regular servants, without having to pay or manage them. He can have whatever meal or refreshment he wants, at all hours, and served up with the cleanliness and comfort of his own house. He orders just what he pleases, having no interest to think of but his own: in short, it is impossible to suppose a greater degree of liberty in living. Clubs, as far as my observation goes, are favourable to economy of time. There is a fixed place to go to; every thing is served with comparative expedition; and it is not customary or general to remain long at table. They are favourable to temperance. It seems that when people can freely please themselves, and when they have an opportunity of living simply, excess is seldom committed. From the account I have of the expenses at the 'Athenaeum' in the year 1832, it appears 'that 17,323 dinners cost on the average 2s. 10d. each; that the average quantity of wine for each person was a small fraction more than half-a-pint.

Such material advantages are often praised in more or less casual references to the Club. Not long after Walker, Prosper Mérimée who was in London in 1837 gave a similar account of the Athenaeum in a letter –

> Mon cher ami, je vous écris assis dans un fauteuil à oreilles de quatre pieds de large, dans une salle de 120 pieds de long, chauffée, lambrissée, dorée, tapissée. A ma droite est un cordon de sonnette, et si je le tire, un homme en habit brun, culotte de velours et bas de soie, montera et m'apportera du thé dans une théière d'argent. En bas, salle à manger aussi grande que le salon, quarante domestiques, comforts, de toute espèce. Mon diner s'est composé d'un plat de poisson délicieux, sauces de dix espèces, un morceau de roastbeef coupé par moi dans une montagne de viande, deux plats de légumes, du fromage et du vin de Xerez; bière à discrétion, le tout m'a couté 4 shillings. Défense de rien donner aux domestiques. L'endroit où l'on voit tout ce luxe et où l'on jouit de toutes ces commodités s'appelle le Club de l'Athenaeum.

It is useful to have this evidence against Voltaire's jibe that England was the home of a hundred religions but only one sauce.

Concentration upon the merely physical comforts and satisfactions of membership is natural, but apart from the use of 'an excellent library with maps', most of those praised by Walker and Mérimée might have been had at a good hotel, although not for six guineas a year. How novel the new facilities were at the time was emphasised by Thomas Walker who, in his essay quoted above, when speaking of men about Town in 1835, said that 'before the establishment of clubs, no money could procure many of the enjoyments which are now within the reach of an income of three hundred a year. . . . Neither the same facilities of living, nor the same opportunities of cultivating society, could have been commanded twenty years since, on any terms.' Much later, Henry James, who in 1878 was elected to the Reform Club, had also enjoyed an honorary membership of the Athenaeum after a similar privilege at the Savile Club, the Travellers' Club and St. James's Club. About the Athenaeum he said, as Mr. Montgomery Hyde reported in *Henry James at Home* (1969):

> When his card for the Savile ran out, John Lothrop Motley, the historian of the Dutch Republic and former United States Minister to the Court of St. James's, 'on whom I had no claim of *any* kind, sent me an invitation to the Athenaeum, which was renewed for several months and which proved an unspeakable blessing'. This was indeed so, since in addition to being able to extend the circle of his acquaintances very considerably, he had the use of what was undoubtedly the best London Club library in

> most congenial surroundings. Here he would repair to dine after a hard day's writing in his lodgings, an additional advantage, since the dinner was 'good and cheap' in comparison with the London restaurants, 'whose badness is literally fabulous.' For Henry the Athenaeum was 'the last word of a high civilisation.'

Mr. Hyde continued,

> Ruth Draper has also recalled an occasion when she called for him one morning at Carlyle Mansions and they went shopping together.
>
> 'On the way – we were going in a four-wheeler – he asked me if I'd mind stopping at the Athenaeum to get a little money, and I shrank back in the back of the cab, having been told that I must never look at the outside of a gentleman's club. Presently he came out and he said: "My dear child, would you like to see the Athenaeum?" I was terrified and very shy and I said: "Oh, Mr. James. would I be allowed to go in?"
>
> 'I was very much embarrassed. He said: "Come with me," so I believe I was one of the few women who has ever been in the inside of the Athenaeum Club. He took me all over the Library and into the room where the beautiful books are and showed me Thackeray's chair and I was duly impressed of course. It was a great thrill.'

Henry James had by then had the distinction of being elected to the Athenaeum under Rule II (1882).

He was not the first American to be so elected. Sir John Cunard, who joined under Rule II in 1852, was the son of a merchant at Philadelphia. John Lothrop Motley was similarly invited to join in 1861. Successive American Ambassadors at the Court of St. James' have regularly been made Honorary Members. American citizens continue to be keen and generous Members of the Club.

In more recent days, Lytton Strachey, who might not be everybody's choice today, was recruited under Rule II in 1931 and W. B. Yeats in 1937. Writing on 18 February of that year to Lady Dorothy Wellesley (*Letters on Poetry from W. B. Yeats to Dorothy Wellesley*, Oxford University Press, 1940, pp. 140, 147), Yeats said 'through Rothenstein's grace, I have been elected to the Athenaeum Club under Rule II (which means no entrance fee); it is, I fear, too expensive for me but as election under that rule is looked on as a great honour I join for a year at any rate. That means that I shall have somewhere to entertain you, for they have a woman's annexe in Carleton [*sic*] Gardens. I have always had a childish desire to walk up those steps & under that classic façade – it seems to belong to folk lore like "London Bridge" & that is my subject.' It was a wish that he was fortunately able to gratify several times in March 1937. In another letter of the 24th of that month he wrote again, saying, 'I am writing in one of the rooms of the Athenaeum library – a famous library. The walls which go up to a great height, but broken by a balcony, all books, and a door invisible because covered with the backs of pretended books.' It would have been the North Library. There is a similar concealed door in the South Library, but that also has two swing doors, glass-panelled. These concealed doors recall the incident at Chatsworth when Lord Salisbury in the Library roused the dozing Duke of Devonshire with the query, 'I say, Cav., how do you get up there?', pointing to a similar balcony to which, as in the North Library of the Athenaeum, there is no visible means of access. The Duke is said to have gazed up at the balcony in some astonishment before he replied, 'I'm damned if I know'. There have probably been some Members of the Athenaeum who have never solved the similar problem there, as they find it simpler to ask the energetic Librarian or her assistants to retrieve any volume they may need that happens to be located near the ceiling.

The utility of the merely physical advantages that a Club can make available in rest, food, drink, facilities for entertaining and so forth, can easily be indicated. 'So forth' includes the Club's barber and the bedrooms on the top floor, the telephone, the possibility of cashing a cheque, and of writing and receiving letters which will be forwarded to absent Members.

In the more leisurely age before 1914 or even 1939 it was possible to play billiards in the Club because two full-sized tables with all facilities were provided below ground. Mr. W. Reeve Wallace who was elected in 1910 remembered that it had been excavated without prior permission from the Crown, an oversight since remedied, of course. There also smoking was allowed long before it was permitted in the Drawing-Room.

Although the Club was from the beginning until after the Second World War, open every Saturday and Sunday, it was no haven of refuge from the rigours of the English Sabbath. Even chess was forbidden. A very early Minute directed that the boards and chessmen were to be kept locked on Sundays. Before Sunday billiards were tolerated in 1927 the Archbishop of Canterbury was consulted, as he was then on the General Committee. The late Mr. Reeve Wallace recalled that he had been asked to move the Resolution rescinding the prohibition on Sunday billiards and that His Grace enquired whether any additional labour would be involved if the game were to be allowed. On being assured that it would not, he said no more and the Motion was carried unanimously. As recorded elsewhere in these pages, the two billiard tables were sacrificed in order that lady guests could be fittingly entertained in a new Annexe. By then the Billiards Room seemed to be less frequented, either because many Club Members seem to have lost interest in the game or because they lack time for diversions such as billiards, chess, and even card games. No longer are the nightly epic battles waged on a billiards table in the famous rooms in Leicester Square between masters such as Inman and others, whose scores were always sure of a few lines in the evening papers.

A Club history affords an occasion to recall the pull that billiards and whist once exerted. In the Athenaeum many hours were given to such pastimes. Billiards was a serious affair. There was a Sub-Committee charged with its oversight. Handicaps, Order, Conditions and Dates of Play, as well as Prizes, were all subjects upon its agenda, to be solemnly discussed and ordered. The Sub-Committee administered funds arising from bequests by keen billiards-players; received gifts and arranged dinners for the players. In the Billiards Room, moreover, were cherished relics, notably the cues of some former members. One such, discovered in 1959, was inscribed 'William Makepeace Thackeray's Billiards Cue 1851–1863'. Herbert Spencer, according to Mr. Tedder, 'played the game as an athletic or hygienic exercise, but always denied the authorship of the story told to the effect that he once said to a junior opponent who beat him that "proficiency in billiards was proof of a misspent life" '. In the History of the Savile Club he is said to have made the same remark there to Robert Louis Stevenson. Spencer's trustees gave his billiard cue and case to the Club.

In later, more dreadful days at the height of the German air-raids on London, the Billiard Room kept alive something of the spirit of Sir Francis Drake. On the night of 10/11 May 1941 the Mayor of Westminster was playing billiards in the Club with Mr. M. T. Tudsbery. The Mayor left after the game for his regular inspection of air-raid shelters, one of which received a direct hit while he was in it, so he died at his post, on duty. Mr. Tudsbery arrived home to find his apartment in ruins.

One or two Members made a vigorous effort to find a room of sufficient size to accommodate at least one of the homeless billiards tables, but it did not prove possible to do so. Today the pressure of life seems to allow little margin for relaxation. A well-known jibe directed against the Athenaeum rather more often than at other Clubs recounts how an elderly Member, deemed to be asleep in an armchair was found after some days to have died, but this like similar witticisms, bears no relation to reality.

The Athenaeum before the addition of the Attic Storey.

Examples of Club Furniture dating from 1830–1840.

The Hall of the Athenaeum, 4.30 p.m., circa 1893.

The eminent writers who have been quoted above were not attempting to analyse or account for all the attractions of a Club that owed its foundation and support to some power over the minds of men that is manifested by their deep regard for literary, scientific and cultural values and traditions. Once successfully launched, as the Athenaeum had been in 1824, it quickly gained momentum by acquiring a standing, an ability to inspire respect, even affection. Members, sometimes their widows and relations, revealed it when they made donations or bequeathed legacies to the Club. On other pages in this book there are brief examples of the way this evidence of a deep attachment to the Athenaeum and all that it represented in national life has benefited the Club and notably its Library. It is as though some special qualities seem able to endow an institution such as a Club for men with an appeal more subtle and far more compelling than the mere physical facilities recited by Mérimée and others quoted above.

CHAPTER THREE

The Spirit of Place

To offer to account for the attraction of a Club by referring to man's 'gregarious instinct', or more poetically to invoke a 'spirit of place' will seem in our modern, literal, matter-of-fact age to be no more than another example of the age-old device of offering to explain one mystery by another that is yet more mysterious. There are nevertheless places that seem to exert a magic spell

> in the very world, which is the world
> Of all of us – the place where in the end
> We find our happiness.

Sceptics who would doubt or scorn any such feelings by seeking to reduce them to their merely material elements are not likely to desist by a poetic adjuration

> Dark brow'd sophist come not anear
> All the place is holy ground.

To invoke such sentiments in referring to so mundane an institution as a Club may seem extravagant until the words of Samuel Johnson on a 'numinous' site are recalled. 'To abstract the mind from all local emotion would be impossible, if it were endeavoured, and would be foolish if it were possible. Whatever withdraws us from the power of our senses; whatever makes the past, the distant or the future predominate over the present, advances us in the dignity of thinking beings.' Whenever a building, or a site on which a famous building once stood or where some famous event took place, is able to exert such influence, there the 'spirit of place' may be experienced by anyone with any historical awareness and imagination.

Even 'sophisters, economists and calculators' can be brought to admit that there is no place like home. It was Hannah More, a very matter-of-fact lady who wrote of

> The almost sacred joys of home,

regarding them as made up of

The sober comfort, all the peace which springs
From the large aggregate of little Things.

A Club is not a home but it can often provide some benefits that a home might not, and so become a gratifying resource that the most dedicated home-lover can value. No man, walking into a bank, office or supermarket experiences the feelings that are usually stirred as he enters his home or his Club. Few men, however learned or experienced, would add nothing to their lives by membership of a good Club. Why this should be so has rarely been fully explained. Those who have had such an experience rarely attempt to analyse it, while those who lack it are unlikely to be curious to know what it is. A valiant attempt was made by Sir Almeric Fitzroy in his *History of the Travellers' Club* (Allen & Unwin, 1927) to 'give space and form to the ideas these dumb stones insensibly embalm'. He found it a baffling task. 'The history of a Club', he said, 'presents no ordinary difficulties to one who ventures to undertake the task of writing it, for the subject is associated with an indestructible *aura*, distinct yet intangible, the force of which is felt from generation to generation, but in no sense susceptible of definition or capable of presentment through the customary vehicles of expression.'

Chief among the many advantages of a more enduring quality are the opportunities that a Club, particularly the larger Clubs, provide for their Members to enlarge their knowledge and enrich their experience of the world on many sides. All the world has always learned from gossip and Members of the Athenaeum are no exception, although they do not emulate the Athenians of old who, according to St. Paul, were singular in spending their time in nothing else but either to tell, or to hear some new thing.

Most Members of the Athenaeum come to it with a rich experience of many countries, with a lifelong interest in many subjects. They are so well informed about the most recent discoveries, inventions and ideas of their day that nobody could fail to profit from them if he had the mind to do so. Most people would wish to do so, at least if Dr. Johnson did not exaggerate when he told Boswell that 'Every human being whose mind is not debauched will be willing to give all he had for knowledge'. Some Members who expected little benefit from membership of the Athenaeum were agreeably surprised. One of the earliest was a Founder Member, Henry Crabb Robinson (1775–1867), a barrister with many literary interests and friendships. In 1824 he recorded in his *Diary*:

Made my first call at the Athenaeum, a genteel establishment; but I foresee that it will not answer my purpose as a dining place, and, if not, I gain nothing by it as a lounge for papers etc.

This was in the very early days, before the Clubhouse had been planned. Commenting on this early opinion in 1851, he completely changed it, saying

It now constitutes one of the greatest elements of my ordinary life, and my becoming a Member was an epoch in my life. These great clubs have changed the character of London society, and will save many a young man from the evils of a rash marriage, as well as habits of dissipation. Originally it was proposed that all Members (1,000) of the Athenaeum should be men of letters, and authors, artists, or men of science, in a word, *producers*; but it was found impossible to form a club solely of such materials, and, had it been possible, it would have been scarcely desirable. So the qualification was extended to *lovers* of literature, and when Amyot proposed me to Heber, the great book-collector, I was declared by Heber to be worthy, on account of my being a German scholar. . . . I was not aware that it would become my ordinary dining place, but I knew it would introduce me to good society.

Again, he recorded that the Athenaeum:

has never ceased to constitute an important feature of my daily life. I had a place of resort at all times, and my circle of acquaintances greatly increased.

Scattered through the biographies, diaries and letters of eminent people in the nineteenth century, are many references to the Club, often casual and scrappy. Much more evidence has irretrievably disappeared, while much of what remains is trivial, fragmentary and difficult to incorporate in a general survey. Fourteen years after Crabb Robinson's first encounter with the Athenaeum, young Mr. Charles Darwin (1809–82) evidently had felt as hesitant as Robinson had been about the likely value of membership to him. Writing on 9 August 1838 to his friend Charles Lyell (1797–1875), the eminent geologist, he reported:

I go and dine at the Athenaeum like a gentleman, or rather like a lord, for I am sure that the first evening I sat in that great drawing-room on a sofa by myself, I felt just like a duke. I am full of admiration for the Athenaeum, one meets so many people there that one likes to see. . . . Your helping me into the Athenaeum has not been thrown away, and I enjoy it the more because I fully expected to detest it.

He need not have been so pessimistic. In 1834 the *New Monthly Magazine* had found that the Athenaeum's

> mixture of Whigs, Radicals, savans, foreigners, dandies, authors, soldiers, sailors, lawyers, artists, doctors, and Members of both Houses of Parliament, together with an exceedingly good average of bishops render the mélange very agreeable, despite of some two or three bores who 'continually do dine' and who, not satisfied with getting a 6s. dinner for 3s. 6d. 'continually do complain'.

In his *Reminiscences* (1910) Goldwin Smith describing his life in London between 1854 and 1861, said, 'blessed are Clubs and above all in my memory the Athenaeum, with its splendid library and its social opportunities. Without Clubs what would bachelor life in London be?'

At this early period already, therefore, the Athenaeum was what it was intended to be, a social-club, and predominantly it has remained so. Naturally it is impossible to imagine all the infinite exchanges at breakfast, lunch, tea and dinner or in Club armchairs, that have enlivened and informed Members of the Athenaeum during a century and a half. Charles Fulke Greville's renowned *Memoirs* give an excellent idea of the topics uppermost in the mind of politically intelligent men in the reigns of George IV, William IV and the earlier years of Queen Victoria. He probably picked up much of it at the Club, although he does not mention the Athenaeum specifically. He became a Member along with Macaulay and others in 1830. Macaulay's *Journal*, when published in full, will be equally valuable as a similar index, but it does not cover so wide a period as Greville's.

Whatever rumour may have alleged about the staid, sober demeanour of Members of the Athenaeum, episcopal or otherwise, their desire for knowledge has not been incompatible with a relish for the lighter side of life. A century, and longer, ago Theodore Hook was able, like poor Yorick, to set at least one table in a roar, but he did not please everybody. Those for whom his wit, humour and practical jokes were too raw, could have had more rewarding encounters with Sydney Smith, 'A Horace to feast with, a Pascal to read'. Tom Moore, the poet, who so described him,

> used to declare that as a conversational wit he vanquished all the men he had ever met . . . 'his wit generally involved a thought worth remembering for its own sake as well as for the brilliant vehicle in which it was conveyed'. Edward Everett from the United States of America was more concise,

> saying, 'If he had not been known as the wittiest man of his day, he would have been accounted one of the wisest.'

His biographer Stuart J. Reid reported in 1896 that

> during the last few years of Sydney Smith's life, the Athenaeum Club formed one of his favourite resorts, and there he might frequently have been seen chatting pleasantly with friends old and new. The chief literary club of the metropolis with its noble library and unusual social advantages, had naturally powerful attractions for such a man and being himself of an eminently 'clubbable' disposition, he was extremely popular within its walls.

Outside them also his invitations were eagerly accepted. On 12 March 1841 he invited Moore, saying, 'I have a breakfast of philosophers tomorrow at ten punctually; muffins and metaphysics, crumpets and contradiction. Will you come?' Who would refuse, apart from the Creeveys of this world?

As in all mixed gatherings those with a lively mind can attract others. They can also repel others. Macaulay's strong dislike of the Club's founder J. W. Croker has already been mentioned. He did not have a high opinion of Southey, but, he said, 'Croker is below Southey, for Southey had a good style, and Croker had nothing but italics and capitals as substitutes for eloquence and reason'. Hook he disliked even more, although he 'could see the merit of the novels of Theodore Hook whom I held in greater abhorrence than even Croker, stuffed as these novels are with scurrility against my political friends'. Hook had been dead for more than twenty years and Croker was also dead when Macaulay wrote these words, but it is not known whether common membership of the Athenaeum softened his animosities.

Apart from political animosities, Hook and Macaulay were inevitably unlikely to agree. Macaulay was no foe to honest mirth or to choice wine, but he would have little sympathy with a man like Hook to whom the words of the Laureate of the Sublime Society of Beef Steaks seem applicable.

> Poets best too, it is said, write and sing when unfed
> But if starv'd I'm undone head and throttle;
> For the pot and the spit are the source of my wit
> And the fount of my fancy the bottle.

The Rev. F. Waugh recorded the following memory of Hook when speaking of the Club's Dining-Room:

> Of the tables, the most historic is, perhaps, the round one at the north-east angle, near the door. At it Hook was accustomed to sit, and from the euphonious designations he gave to the gin-punch and other stronger potations he so repeatedly demanded – asking the intelligent waiters in his gurgling, deep voice for 'a little more toast-and-water,' 'another tumbler of lemonade,' or 'a cup of tea' – the name 'Temperance Corner' survives to this day. Once, on his bill being brought, he noticed he was charged for *ten* glasses of brandy, and objected, declaring he was positive he had 'only nine'. 'But, Sir,' explained the attendant, 'you forget the one you had before you sat down!' The statement, often quoted from the *Quarterly Review*, that after his disappearance dinners fell off to the number of three hundred a-year is an exaggeration.

It was Hook who described the United Service Club as 'the regimental' Club and the Athenaeum as the 'mental' Club, saying of it:

> There's first the Athenaeum Club; so wise, there's not a man of it
> That has not sense enough for six (in fact that is the plan of it);
> The very waiters answer you with eloquence Socratical,
> And always place the knives and forks in order mathematical.

Practical jokes were much more in favour in the nineteenth century than today, and Hook, unlike Macaulay and other Members of the Athenaeum, was much addicted to them, as Waugh also reported:

> A barometer is associated with Theodore Hook's ineradicable passion for mischief, for it was one of his amusements to alter the index from time to time in a somewhat erratic manner. The eccentricity of the instrument thus caused considerable inconvenience to the older Members, who were wont to regulate their 'airings' by the weather-glass; and the committee had to order the key to be removed and kept in the custody of a responsible person.

Hook's behaviour and antics were, therefore, unlikely to appear admirable to Members such as Macaulay, who would not be surprised that when Hook died in 1841, he was oppressed by debt, and, he said, 'done up in purse, body and mind'. He was not a typical Member, otherwise a man such as Cardinal Manning would never have been seen in the Club. Of him Lytton Strachey wrote in *Eminent Victorians* (1918):

> In his private life he was secluded. The ambiguities of his social position

> and his desire to maintain intact the peculiar eminence of his office combined to hold him aloof from the ordinary gatherings of society, though on the rare occasions of his appearance among fashionable and exalted persons he carried all before him. His favoured haunt was the Athenaeum Club, where he sat scanning the newspapers, or conversing with the old friends of former days.

Strachey thus implies that other Members of the Athenaeum after 1875, at least, were neither fashionable nor exalted.

Pages could be filled by other quotations to show that for all the appearance of gravity, dullness or solemnity it may have assumed for some casual observers, the Athenaeum does not deserve the dismal reputation sometimes attributed to it. There are those who, like Poo-bah in *The Mikado*, seem to 'have been born sneering', consequently there is no lack of jibes and innuendos, 'much malice mingled with a little wit', at the expense of its Members. A jaundiced account of the Athenaeum appeared in *Vanity Fair*, an aptly named periodical, on 2 July 1878:

> The Athenaeum is the Club of the unknown and unregarded fogey. In order to insure admission to it, it is necessary to have written a book which nobody will read, or to have done some admirable thing in science or geography which nobody has ever heard of. Superannuated and retired politicians, obsolete authors, disbanded soldiers, antiquated bores, and the general wreck of past generations dine in its halls or wander painfully up and down its steps like whales that have been left stranded by the falling tide.

Fortunately some at least of the Members of the Athenaeum, for example, Macaulay, Dickens, Thackeray, Browning, Henry James, wrote books which some people read, and if the *Vanity Fair* contributor had never heard of 'the thing' done by Charles Darwin, Sir Joseph Hooker, T. H. Huxley, Lord Lister and other scientists, the rest of the world would have been able to enlighten him. More recently, having referred to the ruined Anthaeum at Brighton, Mr. Geoffrey Grigson emphasised that he meant 'Anthaeum, yes; for flowers, not Athenaeum for fossilising professors emeritus [*sic*]' (*Country Life*, 29 February 1968), overlooking the fact that most professors *emeriti* or otherwise very rarely deserve such a label, while his very human literary colleague in the same journal was Richard Church, no fossil, or professor, whose sudden death in 1972 left many of his fellow Members of the Athenaeum very disconsolate.

Bishops have more often been the butt. Professor Sir Walter Raleigh, who strove vigorously after the manner of some men of the book to prove that he was a hearty he-man, neither Christian nor 'fossilising' professor, described the Athenaeum in 1907 as 'this pool of Bethesda of Bishops'. In a similar spirit many years later, he wrote, 'we have plenty of Bishops in the Athenaeum and I am in favour of exchanging them at a low valuation for junior Naval Officers'.

His vigorous spirit made him wish to be on easy terms with men of action in the armed forces. Having been rejected for military service in the First World War, he was eager to get into the war. He became the official historian of the *War in the Air* of the First World War.

It may be here recalled also that when the history of the Royal Air Force in the Second World War came to be written, another Member of the Athenaeum, Philip Guedalla, was asked to write it. He, like Sir Walter before him, died from infections contracted while collecting material for the work. Many are the stories of his bright remarks, still treasured by some of his contemporaries at Balliol and by fellow Members of the Athenaeum. Walking along Whitehall one day in wartime he was asked by a stranger: 'Can you tell me on which side the Admiralty is?' to which he is said to have replied 'Ours, I hope.'

Jokes about Bishops at the Athenaeum were already somewhat stale even in Professor Raleigh's day. When Lord Curzon was Viceroy in India he was amused to learn from a letter that 'Lord Salisbury, it appeared, had been compelled to give up lunching at the Athenaeum because his umbrella was invariably stolen. "It's the Bishops," he said' (D. Wilks, *Curzon in India*, Vol. 2, 1964, p. 102). A variant on this libel recorded the lurid language of a General at the United Service Club who during the annual visitation of the Athenaeum Members in the summer, attributed the loss of his umbrella very volubly in most pagan terms to an unscrupulous Bishop. Umbrellas were so regularly lost or stolen at the Senior, however, twenty years before Athenaeum Members were admitted, that a system of bone checks was tried for a time to protect them. Yet another story recounts that a Member who had lost a fountain-pen asked the Hall Porter to enquire whether a Bishop had taken it, only to be met with the shocked reply 'Oh! Sir, their Lordships make free with umbrellas but *not* with fountain-pens.' Apart perhaps from their benign appearance, Bishops were distinguished from other Members of the Club by their clerical gaiters. That is no doubt why London taxi-drivers after the First World War were said to have improved upon Theodore Hook's description by nicknaming the Athenaeum as 'Bishopsgate' and the United Service Club as 'Cripplegate'. Another Club renowned for the vigour with which some Members expressed themselves, was referred to as 'Billingsgate'. Bishops' gaiters were brought into question in a very irate riposte running into several pages of violent tirade from Captain Pitt-Rivers who had received a mild expostulation upon his entry into the Club one evening in an open-neck shirt and shorts. Insisting with supporting arguments of a varied nature upon his no doubt presumed Common Law right to dress as he pleased, he went so far as to assert that if sartorial oddity was to disqualify, the Committee should consider the appearance of Bishops. Later, Sir Alfred Munnings took without resentment the comment of a Member surprised to see him entering the Club dressed in tweeds at a similar evening hour, 'Have you brought your horse?' Such incidents recall the social climate in which Almeric Fitzroy pronounced that 'no one who has the presumption to dine in morning dress can expect to have his dinner taken seriously'.

In fact, of course, Bishops have always formed a small minority among the Club's membership. Towards the end of the nineteenth century, the Rev. F. G. Waugh gave the following divisions of Members:

> From an analysis made some years since, but still approximately correct, the club appears to be constituted as follows: Law: Judges, 58; Q.C.'s, 35; barristers, 215 – total, 308. Divinity: Bishops, 36; clergy (including 19 dignitaries), 112 – total, 148. Medicine; M.D.'s and surgeons, 82. Making a total for the three professions 538. Universities: Oxford 382; Cambridge, 339; Scotch, 65; Dublin, 49; London, 35 – total, 870. Professors, 74; Societies, Fellows of (chiefly F.R.S.) 269; Royal Academicians, 32; civil engineers, 39; librarians 5; naval officers, 10; military officers, 67; peers, 82; lords (sons of peers), 11; Privy Councillors, 110; honourables 31; baronets, 59; knights, titular, 131; M.P.'s, 59; esquires (including those without affix indicative of degrees, societies, etc.) 760 – total number 1364. The maximum of ordinary members is 1200.

Very different from the views of *Vanity Fair*, Mr. Grigson and Professor Raleigh were those of Mr. David Anderson contributed to *The New York Times Magazine* on 2 April 1944, extolling the Athenaeum as the 'Club of the British Immortals'. He described it as 'at once the most exclusive Club in England and the most inclusive. Nothing quite like it ever happened before; even in London men stand in awe of it.' Sir Eric de Normann valued membership so highly that he declared that time spent there attained 'the summit of human felicity'. It would not be difficult to find others who agree with him. After a sight-seeing tour of London's West End and Clubland in the company of many Americans, the late Mr. A. P. Ryan, a pillar of *The Times*, but not a Member of the Athenaeum, referred to it as 'the monarch of them all'. When assailed by sharp barbs of malicious wit, therefore, Members of such a Club do not lack allies to console them even if they themselves are too modest to attribute envy to their assailants, with the thought that 'envy is a kind of praise'.

Naturally a very rosy view will be taken of the Athenaeum by every Member who relishes his Club, regards its magnificence with something approaching awe, venerates its traditions and respects and admires its more eminent Members and former Members. While he may be amused by jokes about it in the popular Press, he is as little likely to be affected by them, or by the sneers of non-Members, as anyone well acquainted with la belle France would be by jibes about her from people who had never taken more than a day-trip to Calais. A balanced view would show the Athenaeum not as the haunt of desiccated former professors and bishops, the resort of elderly eccentrics; nor as some earthly Valhalla inhabited exclusively by demigods, heroes or their ghosts. Conscious that Members come and go, a 'realist' may think of it as a kind of superior hotel to which admission is restricted by other considerations than the possession of a lot of money; but very much more is involved than that, as it is hoped that these pages may indicate. Human nature being what it is, complete harmony and a general benign feeling of fellowship cannot be said always to have prevailed. Some incompatibilities, such as Croker's hatred of Macaulay, have already been indicated.

Even trivial animosities found an easy outlet by black-balling candidates for election. Hallam, Dean Milman and others were so dismayed by evidence of such feelings in 1840 that they petitioned for the postponement of elections 'in consequence of the unfortunate irritation which at present prevails and the expressed determination of several gentlemen to black-ball every candidate who may be proposed'.

When such a fate could be foreseen, a candidate's name might be withdrawn, as Benjamin Disraeli's was in 1837. He had been entered as a candidate in 1831 by his father Isaac and he was seconded by Thomas Amyot, both popular Members. Amyot had rendered great service in building up the Library. But young Disraeli's youthful extravagances, malicious wit and strong party sentiments had made him too many critics and enemies. 'At your father's Club you are terribly abused', he was told. At that period his biographer described him as a 'raffish, *outré* literary dandy'. (R. Blake, *Disraeli*, Eyre & Spottiswoode, 1966, however, mistakenly said that Disraeli had been black-balled in 1832.)

By 1866 he was Leader of the Conservative Party in the House of Commons, and he had been Chancellor of the Exchequer. He was then easily elected to the Club under Rule II. But he was not a keen Clubman and was rarely seen at the Athenaeum or at any other Club, including Grillion's and The Club, to both of which he was admitted subsequently.

It was not merely on political grounds that feelings could run high. Mean spirits were able to use the occasion to discomfort those they disliked because one black-ball in ten could defeat a candidate. To dilute the effect of malignity the rule was later changed to one black-ball in fifteen. When a purely literary man as eminent as Thackeray was black-balled in 1850, the Committee immediately removed the slur in the following year by electing him under Rule II, against which black-balls in the General Meeting could not prevail. But many excellent men and their sponsors might be left with very sore feelings when, after many years' waiting, a few conspiratorial black-balls could defeat their hopes. Not all of them were as complacent and magnanimous as Thackeray was when he experienced, in the diplomatic words of Mr. Humphry Ward, 'some difficulty about his election'. What Thackeray said was:

> . . . I was quite prepared for the issue of the kind effort made at the Athenaeum in my behalf; indeed, as a satirical writer, I rather wonder that I have not made more enemies than I have. I don't mean enemies in a bad sense, but men conscientiously opposed to my style, art, opinions, impertinences, and so forth. There must be thousands of men to whom the practice of ridicule must be very offensive; doesn't one see such in society, or in one's own family? persons whose nature was not gifted with a sense of humour? Such a man would be wrong not to give me a black-ball, or whatever it is called, a negatory nod of his honest, respectable, stupid old head. And I submit to his verdict without the slightest feeling of animosity against my judge. Why, Doctor Johnson would certainly have black-balled Fielding, whom he pronounced 'A dull fellow, Sir – a dull fellow!' and why shouldn't my friend at the Athenaeum? . . .
>
> If you should ever know the old gentleman (for old I am sure he is, steady and respectable) who objects to me, give him my best compliments, and say I think he was quite right to exercise his judgment honestly, and to act according to that reason with which Heaven has mercifully endowed him. But that he would be slow, I shouldn't in the least object to meet him; . . . my Athenaeum friend has done no earthly harm to any mortal, but he has established his own character and got a great number of testimonials to mine.

Thackeray was more easily consoled for his initial failure to win admission to the Athenaeum because he was thoroughly at home at the Garrick Club, which he had joined as a young man in 1833. Before long he became, according to his fellow Member, Percy Fitzgerald (in his history *The Garrick Club*, 1904, p. 54) 'the choicest spirit of the Club – its centre, its soul, its cynosure. It was his very home, not a mere "house of call" where he dropped in occasionally. It seemed to him to be a sort of whetting-stone for his wit; it kept his humour bright, keen and polished.' It also made him exceedingly sensitive to any slur that might have lowered his standing there. Fitzgerald gave a full account of the way he was provoked by an unpleasant attack on his character by a friend and former crony at the Club, Edmund Yates, into a fury that led him to break with his old friend Charles Dickens. As the story concludes at the Athenaeum, it may be summarised here from Fitzgerald's full account of it. Thackeray and Dickens were both Members of the Athenaeum at the time.

In the summer of 1858, Edmund Yates, a young journalist twenty-six years old, one of the 'gay, pleasant young fellows who were living on their wits in London of the 1850s', had to fill up a vacant column in a weekly periodical *Town Talk*, which he hurriedly wrote at the printer's. It was a far from flattering portrait of Thackeray, his fellow Member, who thought of him as a friend:

> his bearing cold and uninviting, his style of conversation neither openly cynical nor affectedly good-natured and benevolent; his bonhomie forced; his wit biting; his pride easily touched . . .

and more on similar lines, with the additional accusation that he truckled to his audience for gain, praising the Four Georges and the aristocracy of England in his lectures here; damning them in America, where he made George Washington his hero.

Understandably furious, Thackeray sent Yates an angry, scornful letter of protest. Yates is said to have admitted that he had been guilty of bad taste and silliness, but he would neither apologise, nor withdraw from the Garrick Club. Had he apologised there would probably have been no more trouble. Thackeray was sufficiently sure of his standing at the Club to make it the instrument of his revenge. He complained to the Committee. In vain Yates pointed out that his article did not concern the Club, which he had not mentioned, neither did he refer to anything that had happened there. Even if his article had been in very bad taste, the Committee was not an arbiter of taste. He was called upon to apologise or resign. He refused, demanding that the matter should be referred to a General Meeting, which was accordingly summoned. It upheld the Committee, whereupon Yates, who refused still either to apologise or resign was expelled, 'erased' from the list of Members. He meditated a legal action against the Club, but was dissuaded by Dickens, who had advised him throughout, doing his best to heal the breach. Dickens then appealed to Thackeray, asking that he might 'say six words to him at the Athenaeum' and, as arbitrator, effect 'a quiet accommodation of the matter'. 'God knows in no hostile spirit towards anyone, least of all to you.' Thackeray was obdurate, bitterly indignant that Dickens should have espoused the cause of Yates, his friend and editor. Instead of burning the letter, as Dickens asked him to do if he would not agree, he laid it and his reply before the Committee at the Garrick Club. Naturally Dickens resented such a rebuff to his entirely well-meant intervention, with the result that for some years the two old friends behaved as strangers towards one another. The row became the talk of the town. Fitzgerald recalls its conclusion. 'Thackeray was not to live very long, and he and his old friend were happily reconciled in the Hall of the Athenaeum Club, "hard by the coats" – (it *should* have been at the Garrick). The generous Dickens started, hesitated a moment, then put out his hand, which was eagerly seized.' One version depicts Dickens or Thackeray coming down the stairs so the encounter took place 'at the foot of the staircase' but 'the coats' are each side of the staircase, so there is little difference about the scene of this historic reconciliation, which Fitzgerald may have witnessed or been told of by fellow Members who had been there at the time. All such animosities and 'imperfect sympathies' between Club Members can now, as Hook foresaw, be forgotten:

> When Time who steals their wit away
> Shall steal their venom too.

It was not until 1935 that ballotting by the Members as a whole body, that is to say, those of them who chose to attend, was given up; elections thenceforward becoming the responsibility of the General Committee. Long overdue, this change had become the more necessary because the attendance of Members to ballot for the election of new Members had been getting less and less. 'In the last three periods of six consecutive years,' the Committee reported in 1929, 'the average attendance was 235, 169, 141.' In the nineteenth century the Club was sometimes very animated on ballot days, as might be expected when over fifteen hundred candidates were hoping for admission. Within memory some Members sponsoring candidates would stand at the top of the stairs on election days, soliciting the goodwill of Members coming in to vote. 'You may depend on me to do the right thing,' was the response, worthy of the Delphic Oracle, given by one testy Member who disliked being asked to commit himself on such occasions. Failure to secure election has not been unknown in recent years, but if it occurs, it is not the result of a snap vote or the success of anonymous assailants but is impartially decided in the light of as much information as the Honorary Elections Secretary and the Committee can collect about the literary, scientific, artistic or other qualities of each candidate. In electing new Members, 'the right thing' is the Committee's determination to maintain the character of the Athenaeum as a social resort for men known to possess those qualities. Men whose interests lie elsewhere, in business or sport, for example, are likely to be happier in other Clubs, just as most Members of the Athenaeum would be unlikely to feel at home in a Club full of business tycoons.

Anyone endeavouring to compress a history or a description of so unsubstantial a reality as the social 'atmosphere' supposedly characterising a Club that had about 4,500 Members between 1829 and 1887 alone, soon becomes aware how dangerous it can be to generalise on the basis of the few genuinely reliable scraps of evidence that relatively few sources disclose. At best, one or two samples can indicate differences that seem strange today but were probably regarded as normal, right and proper in the circumstances of their time.

At the end of the nineteenth century the Rev. F. G. Waugh gave the following picture of the social life at the Athenaeum:

> Thither resort, day after day, men of intellect and of intellectual tastes, lovers and adherents of literature and art. The scientist, the poet, the philosopher, the traveller, the ambassador, the author, the artist, the theologian, the statesman, the highest members of the learned professions, and those most eminent in naval, military, and civil life, persons of all shades of political opinions, the nobleman, the man about town, and the country gentleman, meet here on a social equality elsewhere unattainable, and enjoy the 'magnetism of personal intercourse'. Foreigners, such as M. Taine and M. Emile de Laveleye, have loudly echoed its praises. He was not so far wrong, perhaps, who laughingly declared that there were few mundane problems likely to present themselves which could not be solved *instanter* by some one of the members to be found between four and six o'clock within the confines of the Athenaeum.

But evidence is not lacking to show that a stiff formality prevailed, at times at least, that inhibited some Members who might have wished to profit by the social opportunities around them. 'A charming place, the Athenaeum', Bulwer is quoted as saying (*Bulwer. A Panorama*, by M. Sadleir, 1913, p. 218n.), 'the

The South Library.

people are so informed; it is a pity they do not know each other. And so very surprising; it is a pity they never converse.' Even then this was probably an exaggeration. When, as Waugh records, over sixteen hundred candidates were on the waiting-list at a time when each would wait about sixteen years for election, none but those with many friends among Members would be admitted. They presumably talked to each other. Nevertheless Bulwer's criticism probably had greater force than it is easy to believe today. At the United Service Club at the close of the nineteenth century, a General who held open the door of a room for an elderly Member with some civil remark was answered by a series of oaths '— you, sir! Can't I walk about my own — club, without being spoken to by a — like you?' So much for the alleged 'gregarious instinct' that is supposed to drive men to form Clubs.

A visitor to London earlier in the present century described the social atmosphere of the Club as solemn. 'I get invited, when I come to London, to the *Athenaeum*, and I am grateful and duly impressed,' said Daniele Varè (*Laughing Diplomat*, 1938/48, p. 242), 'But I agree with Kipling that it feels like entering a cathedral between services'. It would be interesting to know whether the Foreign Office at that time would have made a similar impression. Before 1914 it was said by Ralph Nevill that: 'Whilst club-life, on the whole, has become less formal and ceremonious, a certain number of old-established clubs still maintain a grave solemnity of tone, and such institutions generally contain a considerable number of 'permanent officials' – the class which, whatever party may nominally be in control, really runs the country.' Such men, he said, 'acquire a peculiar look and manner, entirely different from that of ordinary humanity'. As a result 'Many permanent officials – but not those of the Foreign Office, who are generally agreeable men of the world, develop into mere automata radiating a sort of orderly gloom.' Even worse was 'the "retired" permanent official – very solemn and silent, not infrequently pompous, speaking scarcely at all'.

Mr. M. T. Tudsbery, who has given longer and more devoted service to the Club than any other Member since his election in 1924 and to whom these pages are heavily indebted, has recalled the mortification he experienced as a young man newly elected, when he rushed to assist an elderly Member struggling with a heavy overcoat. With the hearty vigour and strength of youth he at last succeeded in getting the coat firmly in place over the old man's shoulders. 'Thank you, Sir, thank you,' the Member gasped, 'You are very kind, but I was really trying to get the thing off.' Mr. Tudsbery confirmed the relative privacy with which members of the Athenaeum once shielded themselves. Anyone desiring to talk to a Member he did not already know was expected, he remembers, to get a Club servant to take his card on a tray asking if he might have the privilege, and refusals were not unknown. Among Mr. Reeve Wallace's recollections of the Club before 1914 was the intense annoyance of an old Member on being asked to introduce another Member to John Morley. All that, said Mr. Tudsbery, was changed during the Second World War. You could not share an Air Raid Shelter or go fire-watching on the roof as relays of gallant Members did every night to extinguish flaming fire-bombs, without breaking down reserve and formality. Members and staff shared the hazards of war. One night Mr. Tudsbery on his rounds found a fire-bomb spluttering on the floor in a service room with an enraged young Cockney pantry-boy cursing and swearing in fluent, unprintable language. He met an encouragement to get a bucket of sand at once by lurid expressions of anguished rage, 'Look at the — floor Sir. I've only washed the — thing this morning.' Mr. Tudsbery fortunately preserved two *jeux d'esprit* from those dangerous days, which indicate that solemnity was by no means the rule. By August 1944 some of the underground shelters used by fire-watchers between alerts had their inconvenient side. One incident drew the following:

Dear Mr. Secretary,

I hate to make complaint:
You say Bunk 2 is comfortable,
I beg to say it aint.
A slat has given way beneath
Some previous occupier –
One's spine now sinks into a pit,
While head and arse are higher.
And then the chap above me made
My prostrate form prostrater:
(Collegii Sancti Petri
Magister Informator
At Westminster – confound the chap!)
Why can't he use the ladder?
Instead of planting horny feet
On me, abaft the bladder.
Tonight I'll risk the flying bombs
And sleep, though nearer Heaven
In every sense.

Yours faithfully,
J.H. (In No. 7.)

A week later the Member inculpated, then the genial Headmaster of Westminster School and later remembered with equal affection as the Master of Jesus College, Oxford, gave his version of the incident. It is hoped that he will now condone its revival.

Dear Mr. Secretary,
I blush with shame
That all through me your bunks should lose their name
For comfort, safety, undisturbed repose
And every boon that every member knows
He needs but raise a casual eye to see 'em
Provided *gratis* at The Athenaeum.
Hear but one plea – if I may make so bold.
'The solemn tongue of midnight' scarce had tolled,
When I descending from my lofty attic
Girt up my loins to leap, all acrobatic,
Up to the perch – I quote your own kind tongue –
'Reserved for those still active, and still young.'
Mark now my words: at that still hour so dread
The bunk below lay all unvisited;
There was the pillow vacant, virgin, neat;
No stertorous form disturbed the unruffled sheet.
Day broke, and rousing from my slumbers' chain
Lightly I leapt to find the floor again.
Ah! what was this, recumbent vague and vast
That, all unknown to me, ere night had passed,
Snatching some hectic moments of repose,
Now heaved its bulk to meet my trembling toes?
A man! I knew it by the muffled curse.
I fled, lest after bad should follow worse.
Guilty, at breakfast-time I scanned the throng:
Who the celebrity had suffered wrong?
A Judge, a General? Prelate, Priest, or Peer?
No face looked more than commonly austere.
Little I dreamt 'neath Hills's glance serene
Lurked outraged dignity and secret spleen:
My plea is made; but, in the name of Pity,
Let not our brawlings vex your great Committee.
On me alone be laid the due disgrace:
The tribe of teachers are a touchy race.
Note, Fellow-members, – and none more than I –
That sleeping Hills, like dogs, are better left to lie.

How very different the nineteenth-century social atmosphere of the Athenaeum must have been from what it has since become is apparent from the recollections in 1956 of Mr. W. Reeve Wallace. His distinguished uncle Henry Reeve (1813–95) whom he well remembered, had known Macaulay, Thackeray and other celebrated men, as well as Charles Greville, whose fascinating *Diary* he edited. Asked by Mr. Tudsbery what, in his memory, he considered to have been the main changes in the Club since his election forty-six years earlier, in 1910, he said at once that the main change had been the admission of guests. Before that 'strangers' who called were shown into a little alcove, now occupied by telephones, where a glass door shut them in. An exception was the possibility of entertaining parties or groups of guests at dinner in a private room providing that at least half those present were Members. The other main change was increased facilities for smoking, but it was only after a long struggle that they were won. In August 1911, Mr. Reeve Wallace recalled, he was talking in the Hall to the first Lord Gorell who lit a cigarette. They were interrupted by a page-boy with a card on a silver waiter. Lord Gorell, thinking that it was a letter, picked it up to find that it bore the words 'Members are reminded that lighted tobacco must neither be taken into the Hall nor into the lift'. They adjourned to the Portico outside. An effort by the Club Committee to change the rule was defeated at the Annual General Meeting in 1928 but not long afterwards the proposal was again made, when it was carried without difficulty.

After the Second World War, when reticence was less of a barrier, the Club was the subject of pleasantry in *The Times* (29 April 1953) in a paragraph reporting

A LETTER FROM BROADMOOR

> From here (Block 6. where reside the 'disturbed class', of whom a few are incorrigibly violent and a threat to all who approach them) there is a continuous gradation to the more stately and formal surroundings of Block 2, the atmosphere of which has been described by someone familiar with both as identical with that of the Athenaeum Club.

On reading it a Member was inspired to provide a rhyming paraphrase with some additional personal reflections. His first six and last two lines ran as follows:

Last night they moved me over here, from 6 to Number 2.
I didn't like them much in 6. They were a lousy crew,

No class and violent! but here – if only you could see 'em
You'ld think yourself at home again, back in the Athenaeum.
The members here are Broadmoor's best. In spite of their mishaps
I'm sure you couldn't hope to meet a nicer set of chaps.

Indeed the social atmosphere's so very like the Club
I wouldn't for the world escape to seek a different pub.

To learn, to be entertained, amused or stirred by some recent gossip may be the greatest good many get from their Club, but it also gives them an opportunity for self-expression, all the more valuable because 'impression without expression' fails to satisfy most natures. Nearly two thousand years ago the Roman poet Martial discovered this after he had left Rome, then the centre of civilisation, to return to his native Spain:

> 'I miss the audience to which I had grown accustomed in Rome,' he said. 'If there is anything pleasing in my small books, it comes from those who listened to me. I feel absolutely stranded now that I lack those penetrating judgements, that fertility of invention, the libraries, the theatres, the social gatherings – all those pleasures from which you learn so much unconsciously and which I fastidiously spurned.'

Many who because of illness, age or for other reasons can no longer drop in at their Club, will have a fellow-feeling with Martial.

Sometimes, it is to be feared, this need for self-expression can produce that stock figure, the 'club bore'. As 'old men forget' and many Club Members are past middle-life, some stories may occasionally be heard more than once. In the Athenaeum, whose Members have mostly had a rich experience of life as well as an agile mind, there is little likelihood that anyone need ever be bored. Much depends on the listener. Few, if any renowned figures of the nineteenth century, have left a greater reputation for an amazing flow of well-informed talk than Macaulay. He was heard at the Athenaeum, not always with the admiration and gratitude that he excited among most of those who made up his usual audience. If even Macaulay could arouse aversion, loquacious lesser men than he find more enemies. 'That kind of club man is the irascible pedant,' said Ralph Nevill, 'whose idiosyncrasies make conversation impossible . . . it was this kind of man who once described Niagara as a horrid place where you couldn't hear the sound of your own voice.'

It is not surprising that an empty-headed social *flâneur* such as Creevey, whose life seems to have been a succession of dinings-out and social tittle-tattle, could describe Macaulay as 'a noisy, vulgar fellow'. Those with an interest in the life of the mind had a different opinion. Greville, who used to join Macaulay's breakfast parties in Albany, spoke of the way 'he loved to pour forth all those stores of his mind and accumulations of his memory to which his humbler guests like myself, used to listen with delighted admiration and enjoy as the choicest of intellectual feasts. . . . I do not believe anybody ever left his society with any feeling of mortification except that which an involuntary comparison between his knowledge and their own ignorance could not fail to engender.' Such was the general verdict. A Club in which a man could hear Macaulay on literature, history, India, the House of Commons and life, as when Thackeray heard him extol the merits of *Clarissa*, must indeed have been a magnet. His memory is not forgotten, or the corner in the South Library where he wrote, for the armchair between it and the fireplace bears a small brass-plate 'Macaulay's chair'. Mark Pattison said that Macaulay's corner was the most delightful place on earth, especially on a Sunday morning. Thackeray and Kinglake were also constantly seen in the Club Library. When such memories become vivid by constantly being recalled by those who have themselves spent hours in the book-lined South Library it will not seem too fanciful a mysticism to invoke a 'spirit of place' as an explanation of the allure of a Club such as the Athenaeum. Commemorating this room in his 'Centenary Record' of the Athenaeum 1824–1924 in *The Times* of 16 February 1924, H. R. Tedder, who had then recently retired, said that it

> is full of reminiscences. Many famous men of letters have worked here. Some portions of *Esmond* were dictated by Thackeray to Eyre Crowe at the central round table at which, in after years, Richard Burton doggedly sat throughout the day, snuff-box at his side, busy at his translation of *The Arabian Nights*; and after him, Andrew Lang, bending over the table, writing for long hours without notes or references. In a corner close to the English history section was the favourite chair of Macaulay, after him frequently used by Hallam, Sir Henry Maine, Matthew Arnold, Mark Pattison and Lord Acton. At the other corner, John Morley, when he edited the *Pall Mall Gazette*, came every day after he had 'put the paper to bed' and sought rest in a large armchair.

This 'South Library' is now dedicated to silence and freedom from tobacco smoke. There Anthony Trollope overheard two Bishops who were discussing his famous *Barchester Towers* voicing considerable distaste for Mrs. Proudie. 'I'll go and kill her off this afternoon', he told them.

Macaulay's Journals in his later years have many references to 'the Club' that seem to refer to the Athenaeum, to which he used to walk after meeting with his fellow Trustees at the British Museum. He was, however, also a Member of the Reform Club and Brooks's, as well as of 'The Club', the dining-club founded by Samuel Johnson.

Naturally those without any enthusiasm for literature will be insensitive to an invocation of memories of these and many other eminent men. What a man gets out of a Club and its Members, as from life and experience in general, is obviously determined in advance to a very large extent by what he brings to it. To any mind willing and anxious to expand, a Club can be invaluable, as John Cam Hobhouse, Darwin, Henry James and others have testified. Mere sensual or worldly folk, and those whose limited experience of life has cramped and confined their universe, lack growing-points in their minds. Those eager enquirers who went to the Lake District, after Wordsworth died, in search of local memories of a man whose conversation Henry Crabb Robinson ranked above that of most of the other literary people he had ever met, gleaned nothing but the most trivial anecdotes from the local country folk. Perhaps Robinson was thinking of these opportunities that Club life provided of associating with great minds when he said that the Athenaeum 'would save many a young man from the evils of a rash marriage as well as habits of dissipation'. Macaulay's example well illustrates the force of that remark because those who heard him heard literature, history and political wisdom speaking; all interests that are inexhaustible and unexhausting; the very contrary therefore to the triviality and sensuality against which all young people have to contend.

When more than material advantages, more than amusement, rest, relaxation, information and a circle of friends and acquaintances are provided by an institution such as the Athenaeum, with its long tradition ably upheld by generations of the leaders of cultural life, it can take on, at least for some Members, a quality that can engage their deepest loyalty, affection, respect and devotion. To reflective souls such an institution embodies, almost emanates, a spirit of its own.

Its values can arise only in a society in which cultural life is honoured. Elsewhere the author has written about the nature of 'culture' as being all that which, transmitted orally by tradition and objectively through writing and other means of expression, enhances the quality of life with meaning and value. It is this inheritance that alone makes possible a development of the human mind towards, first of all, the mere discovery or formulation; next the realisation, appreciation and possession; and finally the personal achievement by constant practice and striving after qualities summarised by those traditional abstract nouns, 'truth', 'beauty' and 'moral worth'. By such means alone is it possible to ensure the perpetuation and the progress of the sciences, of the arts and of worthy behaviour. All who seek relief from the humdrum round of everyday, workaday existence, not to mention the dismal downward vortex of mere sensuality, sexuality and animality, can find it by activities that qualify as 'cultural' in the sense here defined. They may begin on a low or modest level, but however dissimilar such activities may be, they are cultural if they have the common quality of harnessing individual energies on whatever level, in forgetfulness of self, to the attainment of some end deemed to be worthy for its own sake; capable, for them, at least, of qualifying as a form of knowledge, art or humanity. Insensibly these interests forge bonds of union between human beings having similar pursuits, regardless of superficial differences such as those of race, sex, colour or creed. Pursuing this line of thought may help to explain the worth and the appeal that Clubs can make to like-minded people, with substantially shared interests.

Sir Almeric Fitzroy who professed to be baffled by the effort to locate and describe the distinct yet intangible *aura* which he sensed in the Travellers' Club, achieved more in that respect than he at first thought possible. Before he laid down his pen he pointed to 'urbanity, the flower and flavour of intercourse' as 'the root principle of a Club in a settled and polished society'. It was, he said, a spirit that 'imparts a delicate note to the social graces which should distinguish a Club', a Club, that is to say, with traditions of sociability to uphold. Today it may, unfortunately, be felt that there is a somewhat old-world air about Sir Almeric's analysis of the fine flower of an urbane society. Cicero would have understood it, for urbanity was a word he first coined. 'The unity of Club life', Sir Almeric concluded, 'lies in the assimilation of contrasts, the insensible approach by a graduated series of mutual impressions to a common standard of appreciation. Some of these impressions are active, but the most valuable and tenacious, reflective; and these go deepest'. There is an active principle at work. 'By a process of natural selection the atmosphere of a Club tends to eliminate qualities hostile to what is described as a clubbable disposition and to foster those favourable to its growth, among which courtesy, accessibility and tact are most prominent.' This active principle gains in power among Club Members. 'With the expansion of the proper unity of feeling, communal interest acquires emphasis and momentum to the exclusion of those forces which impair confidence and mutual apprehension, with the result that corporate sympathy tends to extinguish personal jealousy and presumption.' Shared cultural interests and attitudes by bringing people together can be seen, therefore, to be potent civilising influences yielding an unsuspected, often unidentified, plus-value over and beyond the ostensible motives, aims or purposes that brought the Club into being; such seem to be some of the powers of that mysterious *aura* of which Sir Almeric Fitzroy wrote. There are those, but they are unlikely to read this book, to whom such intangibles mean nothing. Their attitude recalls the French peasant whose ambitions were limited to 'ma soupe et mon lit' or the *terrae filii*, who, blind to the immense cohesive strength of the national loyalty to the British Crown, snarl at the Royal Family. They provoke the exasperated retort of the eminent psychologist – 'Good Heavens! don't you know what an institution is?'

Any society, school or college where human beings are brought regularly into contact and association gains reputation and standing by its proven ability to develop similar qualities of character and behaviour. Their value to society has been thrown into sharper relief when, as today, such qualities are not only absent from some new institutions but their very opposite has become manifest and has even found advocates. Recent events in the student world, for example, have demonstrated that some new universities and colleges have by no means yet succeeded in realising 'urbanity, the flower and flavour of intercourse', neither can they be credited with 'imparting a delicate note to the social graces of courtesy, accessibility, and tact', as long as such graces are openly flouted there by a noisy minority who are sufficient to besmirch the whole establishment. Mere association for ostensibly cultural purposes cannot quickly convert boors, louts and hooligans into acceptable members of civilised society; a truth which they cannot comprehend and one which the demagogic and anarchic enemies of civilised society have a vested interest in encouraging them not to learn.

This contrast between civilisation and culture and those whom Macaulay and Disraeli feared, 'the barbarians bred within society', is a stark reality in our own time whereas in what is now regarded as the socially more primitive and backward early nineteenth century it did not figure among the motives for founding the Athenaeum and other clubs. It is nevertheless very relevant to their story because it throws their intrinsic worth into high relief, as it also, unfortunately, casts a dark shadow across their future. It is a contrast that should make sceptics hesitate before dismissing as gratuitous mysticism, Sir Almeric Fitzroy's invocation of an *aura* that some clubs seem to possess. And not only clubs, and not only in an English environment.

Under semi-tropical skies and amid African deserts, some such 'aura', some such feeling or sentiment has long been recognised as a potent, very real, and immensely precious force. During his long service in the Sudan and the Middle East, Mr. John Hamilton, a loyal Member of the Athenaeum, who will long be remembered with affection since his death at the end of 1973, learned, among other things, of the power of the 'spirit of place' in North African ways of life and thought. What he there discovered is relevant to the appeal that some Clubs, Colleges and other institutions have long been able to exert. In Arabic, as Mr. Hamilton recorded (in the *Hibbert Journal*, July 1957), the term *báráká* is a regular expression for this abstract quality. It has stimulated and fortified the line of thought followed in these pages which it is well able to carry further. Mr. Hamilton illustrated the idea by his story of the reaction of an old sheik to the Government's intention to bring in a specialist organisation in order to extend by modern methods the irrigation of an area already producing fine crops of high quality grain and cotton. 'You know,' the sheik said to him, 'we do not like this proposal at all. From time immemorial these lands have been our granary and grazing ground and now a company will come and disorganise our life. Although we shall doubtless become richer, how will this benefit us? Our life will be upset, our young men will become demoralised and the *báráká* will go from us.' The sheik was right, for in four years the company had to give up and take concessions elsewhere. Mr. Hamilton was able, having shared the life of the country, to enlarge the dictionary meaning of this Arabic concept of *báráká*, which is 'blessing, happiness, abundance, fertility' by the Christian concepts of virtue and grace.

Mr. Hamilton's story is very relevant in the effort to discover the nature of a club's *aura*, particularly as he developed it by examples from modern life. He quoted from Westermarck's three chapters on *báráká* in which he said that in Africa the horse is 'the noblest of animals and the possessor of much *báráká*', a sentiment still shared by millions in England. The mere suggestion that any such mystic quality can exist in our times of logical positivism, linguistic philosophy and concentration on material values, may seem remote from the real world. Yet many are obscurely conscious that something real but intangible is lost when, for example, in the world of industry the old face-to-face human contacts in small workshops have been superseded by companies and factories in which personal, human relationships between directors, customers and workers hardly exist. Then it is left to new professions of personnel and public relations officers to strive to generate something of the magic formerly automatically arising from and fortifying a satisfying social solidarity.

Every reader alerted to the subtle quality to which these paragraphs allude will however quickly recognise its pervasive reality. Many may realise that it describes sentiments they experience as they see fields and hedgerows destroyed as new motorways, new towns and factories are created; as they contemplate the sordid state of once more agreeable scenes such as Piccadilly Circus and Euston

Station in London. Age or some relation with the soil is not essential as a basis for loyal attachment. A new regiment can rally to its new flag with all the enthusiasm with which the *Alauda* legion followed its silver eagle into the thick of Rome's battles. Quoting Sir Richard Livingstone to the effect that today 'our fundamental need and chief task is to form the right attitude to life, and to give what our age lacks, clear values and definite standards', and Ruskin's urge 'to find under the common thing the hidden grace', Mr. Hamilton was convinced that *báráká* is a concept 'relevant to every facet of our lives – industrial, cultural and social'. Relevant also, as he would be the first to agree, to a Club such as the Athenaeum. 'Any person or thing can acquire *báráká*,' he concluded, 'through a relationship of love and affection.' Remembering the desert sheik's prediction that a rapid, enforced commercialisation that replaces humanity by computerised balance-sheets, will infallibly demoralise, may help to explain the vast social unrest in all 'modern' societies and so bring out much more clearly the need, the duty and the reward of maintaining intact any institution such as a Club with its 'spirit of place'.

It would be unseemly lightly to abandon any way of life, person, place or object to which many have become so attached that they regard it, not only with affection or reverence, but as something which they are prepared to preserve, as others have been before them, at the cost of considerable personal sacrifices. More than mere conservative tenacity is involved. Failure to maintain any such institution would show lack of respect for all the values it represents and all those by whose efforts in the past those values have been created and preserved. 'Far from me and my friends be such frigid philosophy,' said Samuel Johnson, 'as may conduct us indifferent and unmoved over any ground that has been dignified by wisdom, bravery or virtue.'

This brief outline of the origin and development of the Athenaeum throughout one hundred and fifty years will have been written in vain if it fails to convey any conviction that its survival is to be explained not by the ability it shares with hotels, restaurants, public libraries and similar organisations to provide material satisfactions, but by the 'clear values and definite standards' for which it stands; by the loyalties, that it has succeeded in evoking; by its 'aura'; its spirit, its *báráká*.

CHAPTER FOUR

The Athenaeum Library

Foundation of the Library

'Either the possession of, or, in some other shape, access to a far larger collection of books than can be read through in a lifetime, is in fact an absolute condition of intellectual culture and expansion.' This wisdom from that entertaining volume *The Book Hunter* by John Hill Burton (1809–81), Historiographer Royal of Scotland and Member of the Athenaeum (Rule II, 1869) well expresses the determination of the founders of the Athenaeum that their new Club should possess a good library.

Gifts of books poured in from Members to supplement what the Library Committee was able to buy from its annual allocation of £500 from the Club's funds. Two years after the new Club building was opened there were upwards of 10,000 volumes on the shelves. John Murray in whose hospitable premises in Albemarle Street the idea of creating the Athenaeum was said first to have been suggested because of the frequent meeting there of literary men, offered the complete range of all his publications to the Club from which the Library Committee made a large selection which was listed in the Report of 1832. Members then and subsequently were invited to present their writings to the Club which has thereby benefited by some splendid gifts, often made more estimable by having been presented, suitably inscribed by the author. Among them were many of the grand series of thirty-eight large illustrated volumes on the birds of the world, the work of John Gould, F.R.S. (1801–81). He was the son of the foreman gardener at Windsor Castle whom he helped as a boy. His scientific eminence later earned him an invitation in 1854 to become a Member of the Athenaeum under Rule II. These volumes, now very valuable, are among the prized heirlooms of the Athenaeum. Subsequently Gould gave the Club a fine specimen of the Eagle Owl. The Club then already appropriately possessed a 'Temple Owl' sacred to Athens.

When 'an assembly of good fellows' meets under certain conditions to form a Club to aid the life of the mind, and to provide themselves with a good library, the question arises, 'What conditions should govern the choice of books?' When the assembly is of a thousand or more men of various professions and callings, with varying tastes and interests, who moreover change from year to year, and when the original thousand of 1830 become the two thousand of 1974, it is not easy to frame a policy for a collection that would fully cater for all their many and varied interests, particularly when it cannot in any case outgrow the space in which it must be housed. A College in which the courses of instruction provide ready guide-lines for the library authorities, has a much simpler task. Nevertheless the Athenaeum Library has been formed under the guidance of some general principles. They were stated in 1836 by the then Library Committee of seven members in a document said to have been written by Henry Hallam. Their object, it was reported, had been 'to form a collection of useful works in the different provinces of literature and science, without giving any other preference to particular subjects than popular taste, and what they conceive to be the inclination of the members, appeared to prescribe'. Not surprisingly many gaps were indicated, but already in 1836 'almost every standard work of reference' in English History was on the shelves. Generally, 'a principal object' in the formation of the Library was declared to be 'to purchase such works in the fine arts, in Natural History and Antiquities as, though eminently instructive or interesting, are too costly or bulky for the majority of private persons'.

General Character of the Athenaeum Library

A volume devoted to the Library alone would be needed to do justice to the wealth and diversity of its contents. With only some 75,000 volumes it obviously cannot rival large general libraries. (This total was provided by the late Mr. Stirling Boyd and Sir Alan Burns who spent very many hours counting the books on every shelf, using the long cane of a feather duster to deal with the upper shelves. Their total includes the books lent by the Club to Osterley.) It is essentially a working library in the humanities. As a working library, it has been formed by giving priority to the following chief classes of books:

1. Reference works. Encyclopaedias, dictionaries, indexes, foreign as well as English, collections of important statistical material, histories of literature, bibliographies, historical source material particularly relating to Great Britain, from the publications of the Rolls Series and Public Record Office onwards, and similar keys to knowledge.
2. Scholarly texts of the classics of literature, history, philosophy, aesthetics, theology, in English and to some extent in Latin, Greek, French and

German, but rarely in Italian, Spanish or other languages. As complete as possible a coverage of English literature, including, e.g., the publications of the Early English Text Society.

3. Memoirs. Biographical and critical studies of outstanding figures, particularly of Great Britain and the Commonwealth and North America, but not to the exclusion of some of European and other countries, in political, cultural, scientific, religious, and social life when they represent serious works of scholarship based upon original sources or when they are remarkable for their literary merit. The majority of more 'popular' books in this field are borrowed rather than bought.

4. Historical, military, archaeological, and genealogical, etc. works of scholarly and literary merit, particularly relating to Great Britain, the Commonwealth, Europe and North America but not neglecting the best representative studies of other countries. Studies of local as well as of national British history and topography are included.

5. Significant contributions to political theory, law, sociology, and economics, philosophy, ethics, theology, art, architecture, gardens and landscaping, musical history, typography, and the humanities and social sciences generally.

6. Outstanding contributions to science and the history of science and medicine, including geographical surveys and exploration, botany, horticulture.

7. Belles lettres, essays, poetry, although many are borrowed rather than bought.

New books (but not current fiction), are borrowed every month from a circulating library, a practice already begun in the first years of the Club's existence. Several such subscription libraries existed for fiction before young Mr. Mudie began to lend books in 1842 charging borrowers one guinea a year. Sometimes this opportunity to get several opinions on a new book results in its purchase.

Guided by Hallam's principles within the seven main fields indicated above, the Library Committee proceeded to acquire many large works then published in small editions with hand-coloured illustrations such as *Le Case ed i Monimenti di Pompei*, published in Naples in four volumes in 1832; Rosellini's *Egyptian Antiquities*, containing some splendid copies of paintings from Egyptian tombs; the forty-five volumes of the *Thesaurus Antiquitatum et Historiarum Italiae, Siciliae, Sardiniae*, cura G. Graevii et P. Burmanni; and similar works of great erudition and high cost in their day, now seldom, but sometimes still consulted.

Later, other great series were added, notably the fine 'Rolls Series' of chronicles, histories, etc., begun under the direction of the Record Commission and continued by the Public Record Office, with its later majestic Calendars of State Papers and the publications of the Royal Commission on Historical Manuscripts. In 1841 a substantial nucleus of this splendid collection, twenty-nine volumes of the Record Commission, was presented by Henry Hallam, a Founder Member. His munificence, not recorded by Humphry Ward, extended to a hundred other historical books, as well as twenty-nine folio volumes of the early Reports and Papers of the House of Commons, Political, Civil and Military, now very scarce because of the limited number printed and the difficulty of obtaining them when they were first issued, except through a Member of Parliament.

Classical scholars benefit by finding Mommsen's great Corpus of Latin Inscriptions and the *Realen-Encyklop¨die der classischen Altertumswissenschaft* begun in 1894 and completed, save for any subsequent supplements, in 1972, together with the older but still useful French *Dictionnaire des antiquités Grecques et Romaines* by Ch. Daremberg and E. Saglio, 1877–1919. The Club's fine series of all the renowned histories of English Counties is often consulted, together with the modern Victoria County Histories and the richly illustrated publications of the Royal Commissions on Historical Monuments.

In English literature Members expect to find good texts of all well-known authors as well as long series of works published by the Early English Text Society, the Shakespeare Society, the Camden Society and others. In other languages, notably Greek and Latin, all the remaining published literature is available, including the much used Loeb Library. French books were among the acquisitions up to the First World War, but German, Italian and Spanish literature is less well represented. Members are nevertheless often surprised at discovering out-of-the-way books that they did not expect to find on the shelves. Unfortunately the necessity of making space available made many of these books the first victims. A splendid series of French chronicles and historical texts was sacrificed when the Athenaeum lost No. 6 Carlton Gardens.

Dictionaries, encyclopaedias and reference works form the backbone of the collection which is supported by impressive rows of massive folios of the works of most of the Fathers of the Church and later theologians, Erasmus, Calvin and others. The nine volumes of the Amsterdam edition of the works of John Calvin were acquired in 1844 together with seven volumes of Luther's works, printed in Wittenberg in 1545, fifty-three volumes of the *Acta Sanctorum*, 1647–1794, and others. All such monuments of early erudition, many in large folios, may not now be consulted as frequently as in former days but they are retained for the reason John Hill Burton gave for creating a library. After all, of all private and

The Portico and part of the Parthenon-copied Frieze.

The Morning Room

public libraries it is surely true that most of the stock is seldom disturbed. If for that reason books were discarded there would soon be nothing left worth calling a library.

Many are the great values of a Club Library as a working library, not least of them being that a Member can count upon the strong probability, almost certainty, of finding standard and important books in it at any time, after, as well as during the hours that the Library staff are on duty. The Athenaeum, therefore, does not lend books to Members or to anyone else. Rule XLI, quoted below, prohibits the removal of any of the Club's property, whether book, periodical or newspaper, or anything else. None of the Club's books is unique although many would now be very difficult and very costly to replace. By subscribing to the London Library, the Athenaeum is able itself to borrow books for a limited period for consultation within the Library itself, not to be taken away.

Already in 1830 the services of a full-time Librarian were considered essential but an unlucky choice was made by the appointment of the Secretary's clerk who so far betrayed his trust and belied the good reputation he had already acquired and appeared to sustain by diligent service in the Library, that he made off after two years with £200 of the Club's funds. His successor, Spencer Hall, a skilled bibliographer, gave eminent satisfaction, retiring on a pension in 1875 after forty-two years' service, but not before he had trained his assistant Henry Richard Tedder who followed him as Librarian, to which duty that of Secretary was added in 1889. As he did not retire until 1924, two men had oversight of the Library for almost a century.

Not merely the foundations but the main bulk of the Athenaeum Library was created during their long years of service. They did not choose the books. That was the responsibility of successive Library Committees. At first a Sub-Committee of the General Committee of the Club, the Library Committee was given virtually independent status soon after Mr. Tedder's appointment. His intense devotion to the Library and his love of books no doubt gave him great influence, for, as all administrators learn from *The Statesman* of Sir Henry Taylor (1836), if they did not know it already, he who has the task of suggesting action, often is able to get agreement to it, especially from a Committee. Tedder was the more likely to be listened to as he was a thorough, painstaking scholar, as anyone may discover by reading his impressive contribution to the *Dictionary of National Biography* on the great Birmingham printer and virtual pioneer of fine printing in England, John Baskerville. His eminence in the library world led to the Travellers' Club asking him, shortly before he retired, to inspect and report on their Library, then of about 10,000 volumes.

Yeoman service to the Club was rendered by Tedder's successor, R. C. Lambert, who, before he retired on a pension in 1935 after twelve and a half years' service, had by 1931 replaced the old printed and manuscript catalogues of the Library by alphabetically arranged typed catalogue cards, in two series, that of authors and that of subjects. As though Lambert's work had made maintenance of the Library virtually automatic, no Librarian was appointed to succeed him. Sir Stephen Gaselee undertook its oversight as Honorary Librarian with lady assistants. When he died in 1943 the work was ably undertaken, single-handed, by Miss E. Stiff, who served the Club loyally and unobtrusively for seventeen years, retiring eventually in 1962.

Growth of the Library

The Athenaeum Library is managed by its Library Committee which has the task of buying books which may be suggested not only by Members of the Committee, but by Members of the Club at large. A 'Suggestions Book' is provided for this purpose. The first such Suggestions Book, a folio volume of impressive bulk containing entries by eminent nineteenth-century members such as Matthew Arnold and T. H. Huxley, one of whose suggestions led to the acquisition of the Club's set of the works of Hegel, was displayed for inspection when the Club entertained ladies on the opening of their new Annexe on 27 September 1962, after which it has never been seen again, despite a long search for it.

A history of a library cannot recount more than the growth in the number of books it contains; the provision of additional shelving to house them; the problem of disposing of some older books in order to make room for new books; arrangements if any to borrow books; special gifts; losses by fire, war or theft, and the cataloguing and arrangement of the library's contents.

How the Library has grown is immediately visible from a tour of the shelves. At first all the books were in one room – the Library, with bookshelves half-way up the wall. It is now the 'South Library', still the largest of all the book rooms. Since 1830 it has been doubled in size by shelves up to the ceiling and the installation first of one gallery by Burton in 1832 with an iron staircase giving access to a platform running all round the room. He was then called upon to design and install bookshelves in the Drawing-Room. As the years went on, bookshelves were fitted around more and more rooms. In this way the North Library was created and that also was provided with an iron gallery. The West Library was filled from floor to ceiling; bookstores were created on the Mezzanine floor and the South Library was provided with an upper gallery, more stairs and another platform. The new large Card Room running along the whole of the south side of the Clubhouse which was created when the third storey was added was also soon lined with books. Still the Library grew, overflowing into the basement and any available space. From the original 10,000 in 1832, the number of volumes in the Library rose to 20,000 in 1844 and over 30,000 in 1850.

Gifts and Bequests

For many years after 1831 the Committee's Annual Report to the General Meeting of the Athenaeum printed long lists of gifts to the Library. 'The great liberality manifested by many of the Members of the Club in presenting books to the Library' was often acknowledged. In May 1832 the first long list is believed to record all books presented since the Club began in 1824. Among them were those given by Mr. John Murray from his vast stock. Captain Christopher Clarke of the Royal Artillery was one of the first to send a considerable collection of works of historical interest and books of travel between 1824 and 1831 and in the following years. Sir Parish Woodbine in 1837 gave the Club eleven volumes of pamphlets on various subjects and four volumes of Tracts on America, so laying the foundation of that large collection of ephemeral publications of a past age which are now to be found with difficulty and usually only in large libraries, and which constitutes one of the most valuable single sections of the Club's Library. It is remarkable for the light it throws on social, economic and cultural history. Many seemingly new controversies will be found to have been anticipated by our predecessors. In the same year, 1837, in which Sir Martin Archer Shee's observations *On the Claim of the Public to be admitted 'Gratis' to the National Gallery* were presented to the Club so was George Rennie's reply *Observations in Reply to Sir Martin Archer Shee on Admission to the National Gallery*, both of which were preserved and bound in the Pamphlet Collection. Naturally not all the gifts were of the same value. The Reverend Christopher Benson's Sermon on *Israelites asking for a King* presented in 1832 may have arrived before the Pamphlet Collection was begun, because it is not now to be found in the Club, although nine other of his works are in the Pamphlet Collection. It seems plausible to believe that the Librarian, Spencer Hall, newly appointed in 1833, was responsible for instituting that series.

Gifts came from American Members and Honorary Members. Edward Everett, one of that renowned company of distinguished and eloquent orators bred in the United States in the first half of the nineteenth century, was generous in presenting pamphlets, fortunately preserved. Other gifts from America still on the shelves include Ambassador Richard Rush's *Memoranda of a residence at the Court of London* printed in Philadelphia in 1837. In subsequent years the Club was to benefit remarkably by similar munificence, particularly since American scholarship has devoted such vast resources to the study and publication of the classics of English literature. However much political, economic and material interests may diverge, this common heritage constitutes an abiding special relationship in the world of culture in which distinctions based on nationality, sex, race, and even religion will, for its devotees, prove irrelevant or of minor significance.

A bibliophile would find it fascinating to compare the lists of early gifts and the early catalogues begun with exemplary zeal by Spencer Hall, with the present catalogue. The extent to which the Athenaeum has been able to retain many of the volumes of its original Library would then be evident. Many have had to go, as they have to go in all but large national collections. In 1882 the first of half a dozen entries appears among the 'miscellaneous receipts' in the Club's annual accounts in respect of 'duplicate and obsolete books' but the total sales in the 1880s realised under £110. They then ceased for many years.

It is also evident that the volumes in the Librarian's charge were well cared for; annual payments of £25 occur in the accounts in 1875 and subsequent years for cleaning, while the money spent on binding and the repair of books was rarely less than £150 a year and often half as much or more of the money spent on bookbuying. These sums were, of course, in golden sovereigns.

Gifts of money were also made, the earliest being recorded in the early days of the Club from David S. Hewson, Esq., of five guineas 'for the Library Fund'. In 1853 the Rev. Charles Turnor bequeathed £500 for Library books, part of which was used to acquire seventy-seven volumes of that extraordinary publishing achievement of l'Abbé Migne, *Cursus Patrologiae*. By 1859 all the money had been spent. Ten years later Felix Slade, Esq., gave £200 to the Librarian for books on art.

Pages could be filled with accounts of notable additions throughout the nineteenth century. In more recent times an exceptionally valuable donation was of four hundred volumes in 1908 by the Hon. W. W. Vernon, the well-known Dante scholar. It did not, however, exhaust the Vernon Dante Library because the Travellers' Club next door received a similar gift in 1917. In 1972 a hundred fine modern volumes, mainly very well-illustrated books on archaeology and art, were presented by F. W. Guy Hamilton who has been Chairman of the Library Committee and has for many years given devoted service to the Club.

The regular flow of books has in recent years included some lavish and costly volumes in addition to those given by Guy Hamilton, such as those given by the late Sir Frederick Leith-Ross and the excellent facsimile reproduction of the famous medieval manuscript, the Trinity College *Apocalypse*. That volume announced in 1965 at a price of £126 was ordered as a gift to the Club by Sir George Wilkinson. In addition to presents of books there have been substantial gifts of money to be spent at the discretion of the Library Committee, particularly for the purchase of books that would otherwise be ruled out of consideration because of their high price. In 1956 Mr. F. J. F. Barrington; in 1968 Mr. T. Stirling Boyd; and in 1969 Sir Hugh Dow made exceptionally generous endowments. Bookplates with the Club's crest were specially engraved to commemorate their generosity. They are therefore fittingly and permanently associated with some of the most notable modern books in the Library. Their gifts aided the Club at a time when a swift decline in the value of sterling, unprecedented since the debasement of the currency by the early Tudor kings, caused a sharp and continuing rise in all costs, those of books included. Henry Hallam's proposal of 1836 that the Athenaeum Library should acquire 'eminently instructive or interesting books that are too costly or bulky for the majority of private persons' takes on a new and more extensive significance in these days when inflation has caused the price of scholarly books to soar, thus limiting their sale and further increasing their unit cost. In Hallam's day, moreover, many of his fellow Members had spacious town and country residences instead of the present-day almost bookless small apartments and country cottages into which people are now driven by confiscatory taxation and inflated rents and rates, as cultural life and all that by which it is sustained – books, pictures, fine architecture, music, libraries, museums and galleries, Colleges and Clubs – suffer the disastrous effects of inflation.

Discarding Books

Members of the Club regard themselves as trustees of a valuable heritage which it is a duty to safeguard, to improve and to transmit. Because of the inherent, intrinsic worth of many books their value tends steadily to grow greater as more people throughout the world come to appreciate their worth and so desire to possess them. Any library, such as that of the Athenaeum, selected with care by men of good judgement in their time, takes on a special character notable both for the quality of most of the books in themselves and for the fact that, obsolete or not, they broadly reflect the state of British cultural life as it has developed during a century and a half. It must therefore be with the greatest reluctance that any books are discarded. Some such as duplicates and superseded annual reference works must go as new books are acquired. Other standard works are sold as more scholarly texts become available, unless there are good reasons for retaining early editions because of their inherent interest or value or because they have so frequently been cited in other books, or on account of some association of the author or editor with the Club. Members are encouraged to present books to the Library. They are unlikely to respond favourably if they see books previously presented among those discarded.

Mainly in order to free shelf-space, the Committee in 1945 gave 'certain sets of periodicals', many of them incomplete, 'to war-damaged Libraries, the British Museum, the Victoria and Albert Museum, the National Central Library and the Inter-Allied Book Centre that had been established to collect in England as many books as possible to help to restock pillaged and devastated libraries of Great Britain's Allies in the Second World War.'

Many feet of shelving were liberated when, in response to an appeal from the Director of the Victoria and Albert Museum, several hundred decoratively bound editions of the classics and other large folios were loaned to furnish the library at Osterley Park. Any volume so lent is returnable on demand. As the story of the Ladies' Annexe recounts, several thousand volumes were stored there until the Athenaeum was evicted because the Crown Estate Commissioners had decided to exploit the site commercially. Such was the bulk and value of the books to be sacrificed in 1960–1 that when they were sent to the auction rooms they realised several thousand pounds.

Newspapers

One of the attractions of the eighteenth-century coffee-house was the opportunity that the best of them provided to read the newspapers of the day. 'Newspapers always excite curiosity,' said Charles Lamb who lamented, 'what an eternal time that gentleman in black, at Nando's, keeps the paper. I am sick of hearing the waiter bawling out incessantly "the Chronicle is in hand, Sir".' (Nando's was a coffee-house, founded in the seventeenth century at the corner of Inner Temple Gate, No. 15 Fleet Street.) At the Athenaeum from its earliest days Members expected to do better. Here is the list of 'Papers taken' by the Club in 1833:

	Daily, morning		*Daily, evening*		*Sunday papers*
3	Morning Chronicle	4	Couriers	4	John Bulls
2	Guardians	6	Globes	3	Ages
3	Heralds	2	Suns	2	Examiners
2	Morning Post	5	Standards	2	Observers
4	Times	4	Albions	1	Sunday Times
14		1	True Sun	1	News
		22		1	Atlas
				1	Spectator
				1	Alfred
				1	Bell's Messenger
				17	

Provincial
Cambridge Chronicle
Oxford Journal
Dublin Evening Mail
Edinburgh Courant
Scotsman
5

American
Viles Register

Foreign
Journal des Débats
Gazette de France
Constitutionnel

Most people will probably be surprised to hear that in 1833 the Athenaeum provided its Members with three times as many newspapers as it does in this 'age of affluence' when there are twice as many Members and when the price of newspapers is very much less (in gold) than it was in 1833. When sailing-ships brought newspapers from France three French papers were taken. Today (1974) there is only one.

In the nineteenth century there was a great development of general and specialised periodicals, weekly, monthly and quarterly; a number of them being the organs of learned societies.

Periodicals and Learned Journals

A Club, like a College Common Room, is a place where Members expect to be able to find current and recent issues of a number of specialised journals. Members of the Athenaeum in common with scholars everywhere now rely heavily upon them. Nowadays the pace of discovery and the flow of new ideas is such that it is impossible to keep up to date in any subject through printed books alone. Publication difficulties and production delays now seem more than ever before to retard the rapid presentation of new ideas by the traditional means of the printed book. Consequently the Athenaeum subscribes for learned and specialised journals devoted to agricultural and rural affairs, architecture, the arts, literature and criticism, bibliography, classics, education, geographical and regional matters, history and archaeology, law, medicine, music, philosophy, politics and economics, religion, science as well as about a score of general magazines. They are all periodicals in the English language with the exception of the *Revue Historique*, *Historische Zeitschrift*, *Revue des Deux Mondes* and *Le Monde*. A number of Members subscribe for periodicals to be presented to the Library, a valuable addition to the Library's resources. Nowhere but in such a well-furnished Library is it possible to capture at least some of the spray from the roaring Niagara flood of the printed word.

Among the prized resources of the Athenaeum, its remaining collection of bound sets of periodicals certainly deserves special mention. Beginning with the learned journal that holds the record for the longest continuous publication, the Club is fortunate in possessing all the *Philosophical Transactions of the Royal Society* from its first appearance. Other notable bound sets of learned journals include:

Athenaeum, 1832–1920
The Quarterly Review, 221 volumes
Edinburgh Review, 257 volumes
Gazette des Beaux Arts, 156 volumes
Almanach de Gotha, 86 volumes
Antiquaries Journal, 1921–
Antiquity, 1927–
Economic Journal, 1891–
Speculum, 1926–
Revue Historique, 1875–
Mind, 1876–
Notes and Queries, 1849–
Journal of the Royal Asiatic Society, 1835–
British Archaeological Journal, 1845–
English Historical Review, 1886–
Punch, 1841–

Journal of Roman Studies, 1911–
Journal of Hellenic Studies, 1880–
Nature, 1870–
Classical Quarterly, 1907–
Classical Review, 1892–
Law Quarterly Review, 1885–
Burlington Magazine, 1902–

Members have the great advantage of being able to consult these valuable sets at any time instead of endeavouring to track them down in some large library. To these sets, most of them being complete from Volume I to the present time, or to the year in which they ceased publication (the first five listed have so ceased) should be added the Official Report of the Proceedings of Parliament, Lords and Commons; the Parliamentary Debates or 'Hansard' as they are usually described. At least one former Prime Minister had their aid in recent years when he was writing his reminiscences.

Theft and Mutilation of Books and Periodicals

A disagreeable aspect of the history of all libraries, including those of Clubs, has always been the losses sustained by theft. A particularly bad instance occurred at the Athenaeum in 1846 when it became evident that volumes were disappearing from the Library shelves. It was discovered with police aid that a Member had been regularly stealing books and selling them to booksellers, 'a solitary and painful incident in our annals' commented Humphry Ward in 1926. As may be expected, the Club's Rules are explicit in defending the Club property. Every Member, as a condition of being admitted, is unequivocally committed to respect all such property and in particular, never to remove a book, newspaper or periodical from the Club premises.

Rule XLI states:

> No member shall take away from the Club, injure or destroy any newspaper, pamphlet or book or other article which is the property or in the custody of the Club.

In spite of so explicit a condition and warning, the Club had hardly opened its doors before the Librarian reported in 1832 that a number of books from the Circulating Library and from the Club's own shelves were missing. Newspapers also disappeared, 'the *Age* is a constant victim', he said. In vain the strongest warning was issued threatening all pilferers with 'immediate expulsion'. In 1840 the Librarian was still complaining that French novels 'were being frequently abstracted from the Foreign Circulating Library'. No such fears can arise today because Members of the Club do not seem to have sufficient leisure or interest in French novels, which is just as well, because there is no 'Foreign Circulating Library' in London from which they may be borrowed. In the middle of the nineteenth century foreign books were obtainable from at least three circulating libraries, the British Library, Rolandi's (which cost £3 for twelve books) and Mudie's, which alone continued until it also collapsed in 1937. Circulating libraries no longer flourish; they amalgamate and disappear more completely than Clubs have done, both examples of the change in cultural life, or the lack of it, that still awaits adequate explanation. Naturally the Athenaeum's finances had to make good any losses from a circulating library. Members who would not dream of filching money from a till, were in effect doing just that, and indeed worse when they abstracted volumes that other Members may have wanted to read. Such was *Illustrations of the Passes of the Alps* by William Brockendon (1827), a large folio which vanished from the shelves in the early days of the Club and in the early days of a growing interest in visiting mountains. Such immorality was notable not only in the Athenaeum which as a Club for 'gentlemen', as Croker designed it, eminent in literature, art, science, law and the Church, might have been thought immune.

In 1877 the United Service Club, alarmed 'on account of the constant loss of books, decided to have a label with the "device" of the Club pasted inside the cover. Many complaints were received of Members hiding the circulating library books. This however had been going on for sixty years' and, the Club's historian added in 1937, 'it still goes on'. Similar protective labels are pasted inside the cover of the books at the Athenaeum and in addition its seal is impressed in gold on the spine of the books. They now also carry the Library classification number lettered on the spine.

Continuing losses of books from the circulating library reached alarming proportions between 1938 and 1942. By 1942 out of seventy-five volumes borrowed, fifty had disappeared. Thereupon the Library Committee ordered that all the borrowed volumes should be kept under lock and key and that any Member wishing to read them should sign a receipt for them. A similar practice has been tried in other Clubs subject to the same depredations but it has the great disadvantage that Members are unable, as they naturally wish, to browse among the new arrivals before selecting one to read. When the Library staff have left for the day it is impossible to get even one, which is frustrating for Members spending an evening in the Club or staying the night there. So the risk of leaving all the borrowed books on an open shelf was again taken. Within a few years the thefts recommenced. In one year the Athenaeum had to pay, in addition to its subscription to the lending library, the cost of twenty-three missing volumes out of the sixty-three it had borrowed. That is to say that one or more Members made his fellow Members buy books for him. When by the following April a further fifteen were missing, and when moreover out of eight copies of *The Times*, then delivered every morning, seldom more than one remained by 6 p.m.; when weekly periodicals shared a similar fate, and when articles and illustrations of general interest were cut or torn out of papers and magazines, the Club Committee circulated a stern warning denouncing both the breach of the Club's Rules and 'a practice scandalously selfish and most detrimental to the social life and amenities of the Club'. This particular circular provoked a slim quarto with illustrations *de l'époque*, '*The Strange Case of the Megatherium Thefts.* A further memoir of Sherlock Holmes, edited from an unpublished M/S of Dr. Watson by S.C.R.' Those initials did not disguise the well-loved Member who since 1936 had enlivened the Athenaeum, as he had already cheered Pembroke College, Cambridge, and the world at large by his studies of the eighteenth century and by narrating the fate of Zuleika Dobson at Cambridge. For that he earned the thanks, among others, of Max Beerbohm, who confessed that he had often wondered what happened to her there, but 'now,' he said, 'I know'. Sherlock Holmes overheard during his visitor's altercation with the cab driver that the hansom had brought him from Waterloo Place, so he did not find it difficult to conclude from the professional appearance of the man that he had not come from the United Service Club, but from the one opposite, the 'Megatherium'. Despite the success with which the detective of all detectives divined the identity of the culprit of the crime he had been asked by his visitor to solve, of stealing the Club's volumes from the circulating library, a feat resulting in the restoration of the missing volumes, Mr. Holmes could not prevent a recurrence of the outrage. No more than 125 copies of his absorbing story were printed 'for private circulation'; insufficient therefore to inoculate more than ten times that number of Members of the Megatherium against the subtle virus of larceny. Other measures had to be tried, without the aid of Sherlock Holmes. In 1960 after further 'repeated losses' over the years the Library Committee suspended, amid protests, the circulating library subscription for a few months. When it was restored the losses ceased for a time.

Less financially burdensome than the theft of books, although often as exasperating, is the theft of newspapers and periodicals. All are overstamped, clearly indicating that they are the property of the Athenaeum, not to be taken away, but depredations have unfortunately continued. The vexatious practice recurred of the removal of pages containing some article or illustration of special interest.

Of all the enemies of books and readers, the book-thief is the nastiest. Why otherwise honest, worthy folk demean themselves by such robbery, remains a mystery which they themselves could not explain. Long before books were printed, when manuscript volumes in any quantity were hardly ever seen outside monasteries, stringent rules were made to safeguard volumes but there seems no evidence from medieval Europe to support the practice in some Indian libraries today, alleged to rest on medieval precedents, of making librarians personally responsible for all loss or damage to volumes in their care. However, the unfortunate William Below (1756–1816), prominent in the Alfred Club, was dismissed from his post of Keeper of Printed Books in the British Museum in 1806 because he had trusted an unscrupulous person who was detected stealing books from the Library. Not many librarians would long retain their appointment if this Indian rule were to be applied today. Book thieves have distinguished, most exalted predecessors, not counting the legions of those who 'borrow' books, never to return them. Pamphilio, later Pope Innocent X was caught redhanded when he stole a book from Cardinal Barberini which is said to have provoked his persecution of the Barberini family later. Another Cardinal, also later a Pope, stole a book from Ménage. There is, therefore, as Mr. Holbrook Jackson (an Athenaeum Member) said in his absorbing work *The Anatomy of Bibliomania*, 'abundance of evidence to prove there is ample reason at all times for such precautions as have been taken against biblioklepts, pilferers, embezzlers, borrowers tardy of redeeming their trust and other bookish malefactors, rogues and depredators, and to strive to confute their folly and madness, and to reduce them *si fieri posset, ad sanam mentem* to a better mind, though to small purpose many times'.

In 1972 a concerted effort against book-thieves was planned in London to unite librarians and booksellers so as to make it difficult for stolen books to be sold without detection. Because the market for rare books is now worldwide, it will obviously be desirable to establish international links, because so much property stolen in Great Britain is now clandestinely exported.

On more than one occasion the Athenaeum has been able to recover some missing volumes after the death of a Member whose executors or heirs report that the books had been found among the late Member's effects. News about any book that seems to have been unlawfully removed from the Athenaeum would be welcomed by the Librarian.

The Athenaeum Library Re-catalogued

As in any Library founded before the more scientific classification of books had been invented, the arrangement of the Athenaeum's books was inevitably somewhat haphazard, seemingly influenced to a considerable extent by the availability of shelving of suitable height for the books. Soon after Spencer Hall became Librarian he printed 'for private circulation only', in 1838, *Suggestions for the Classification of the Library now collecting at the Athenaeum.*

By the end of the nineteenth century progress had been great. Some effort had been made to group books with reference to their contents. Numbered and lettered shelves with a key plan to their location, combined with card indexes of authors and subjects, enabled Members to locate and usually to find the books they needed without difficulty. In 1964 the Chairman of the Library Committee, Sir Alan Burns, who has consistently, persistently and successfully championed the Library, announced at the Club's Annual General Meeting that it had been decided to reclassify it on the system devised by the Library of Congress of the United States of America. He did not mention his own contribution which was to prepare and type out a series of subject lists of the books in the Library. Owing mainly to staffing problems, neither the then Librarian, nor her successor had been able to make much progress. The completion of the work was left to the next Librarian, Miss Jane Clark, appointed in October 1968, who had joined the Club as Assistant Librarian in November 1967. Only those who have had an experience of classifying books and moving them to other shelves will appreciate the magnitude of the task and the sheer physical labour undertaken by Miss Clark and her assistants. So wholesale a migration of volumes from shelves where Members had always previously found them not surprisingly caused some annoyance, for Clubs are conservative, it has been said, as the sea is salt.

Bookbinding and the Care of Books

Few except those responsible for the care and upkeep of a working library in daily use become vividly aware of the fact that, just as working clothes, gloves and shoes wear out, so also do bookbindings. In the thirty years between 1883 and 1913, when binding was relatively inexpensive and relatively quickly carried out, the Athenaeum spent nearly £4,000 (gold) on the binding and repair of books in the Library. Nearly £700 was spent in the same period on dusting the Library, before the days of electric vacuum-cleaners. Two world wars halted or greatly delayed all such rescue work. When the work of reclassifying and re-arranging the whole Library was undertaken in the 1970s many volumes were discovered to need repair or rebinding, both processes now much more expensive than formerly as a result very largely of the depreciation of the currency through inflation, and of the scarcity of skilled binders. Nearly £600 was spent in 1970 on binding alone and more than that amount in the following year, so reducing the sums available for new books and involving the Librarian in a great deal of additional work. Many old leather or vellum bindings have been cleaned in recent years by the Library staff.

Pictures and Portrait Busts

Unlike some clubs, the Athenaeum has little wall space free from bookshelves, so its pictures are not as numerous as they might have been. Not all of the few portraits are of Members. Dr. Johnson, by Opie, for instance, hangs in the Morning Room. A likeness of Frederick the Great, which Carlyle praised as the best, was among other gifts to the Club. But for a decision of the Club Committee, the more extraordinary because it was recorded as having been taken 'unanimously' as well as having been approved at the Annual General Meeting in 1857, the Club would still possess a splendid picture by Sir Thomas Lawrence, one of his flattering portrayals of George IV. It was the last picture to be painted by that Founding Member of the Athenaeum, which he finished, so it was said, a few hours before he died in 1830. His intention had been to give it to the Club, but his executor charged the Club £128. 10s. for it. Commenting upon the Athenaeum's new building, the *Gentlemen's Magazine* reported in March 1830 (Vol. 100, p. 351), 'Over the Fireplace of the Library is an empty space, once destined by the Committee for the reception of Sir Thomas Lawrence's picture of the King, but which is now positively refused by the Executors.' A large mirror was placed there instead, until the picture was bought in 1831.

After hanging in the Coffee Room for a quarter of a century the picture was taken down and ultimately presented to the Corporation of Brighton. No reasons were given. It now seems strange that so excellent a work of art, painted by a renowned Founder Member could have been alienated from the Club nearly thirty years after the artist and the King had died. It was presented to the Corporation of Brighton on the understanding that they would have it hung in the Royal Pavilion, but it is now to be found in the Art Gallery which did not exist when the presentation was made.

Some pleasant water-colours presented by Members adorn the Ladies' Annexe, and there are a few elsewhere. If distinguished artists and sculptors had been invited, as authors were from the beginning, to present at least one of their works, the Athenaeum would have inherited a more distinguished collection of pictures of the nineteenth century onwards than any other Club could boast. J. W. M. Turner might head the list, for he was an early Member. In his Centenary Record of the Athenaeum contributed to *The Times* of 16 February 1924, H. R. Tedder recalls that:

> the South West corner of the Coffee Room was the customary seat of J. W. M. Turner who used to dine alone, and, after dinner, order the candles to be taken away so that he might consume in darkness a bottle of port by himself.

Two eminent painters did not disdain the task of interior decorating. Sir L. Alma-Tadema was responsible for the glowing marble panels in the hall and round the grand staircase. They posed a colour problem very happily solved by the choice of a matching colour scheme and pattern when it became necessary to renew the large stair-carpet in 1971. He also 'designed the beautiful coloured ornaments in the wagon roof and on the ceiling' as well as 'the coloured ornamention' of the Drawing Room. 'The Pompeian decoration of the Coffee Room' that Tedder mentioned, so reminiscent of Alma-Tadema's classical interests, was not his work, however, but that of Sir Edward Poynter. It is no longer visible, having been obliterated when the room was redecorated some years ago.

When the decision to take this step became known there was violent opposition which the Committee patiently answered by showing that their decision not to attempt to restore the work of the two distinguished Royal Academicians was not taken on aesthetic grounds, but was forced upon them because the plasterwork was crumbling beyond restoration, except at ruinous cost. Sir John Summerson supervised the redecoration.

George Richmond who had already given five volumes of engravings of his works, gave twenty-one proofs of some of his engraved portraits to the Club in 1884. Other engravings and etchings, including some splendid examples of Meryon's work, were bequeathed by Colonel F. A. Lucas in 1918. The Athenaeum Committee refused in 1886 to accept an offer from the Society of Dilettanti to deposit their fine collection of portraits of their past Members with the Club if they could be allowed to dine there on six Sundays in the year. Although the Committee were supposed to have examined the proposal 'with the best will in the world' they 'regretfully found that the scheme was impracticable, and negotiations soon dropped'. When it is recalled that Sir Joshua Reynolds had been one of the Society's official painters; that he painted two famous groups of Members as well as some of the portraits which every Member of the Society was required to present to the Club on election, a lament that the Committee did not show more enthusiasm towards the Society will not need emphasis.

Among other works of art the Club is fortunate in possessing some excellent marble and other busts of distinguished Members. Two of the most striking are not of Members. One is of Dr. Samuel Johnson, a fine head in terracotta in the South Library, presented by Percy Fitzgerald, one of Boswell's many editors; another of Alexander Pope, by Rysbrack, is a splendid bequest to the Club.

Other notable busts are those by Chantrey of the Club's Founder, John Wilson Croker; Lord Leighton, a massive and impressive bronze by Brock; Sir Walter Scott and John Milton. Most Clubs accumulate miscellaneous treasures and mementos bequeated by Members, and the Athenaeum is no exception, but it is to be feared that they rarely attract much attention. The 'empty chair' from Gadshill used by Charles Dickens, and Faraday's wheelchair, both remarkably appropriate and generous gifts, are perhaps exceptions because they are larger and more prominent than the seals, coins and snuff-boxes exhibited in a glass case. There are preserved, for example, the original seal designed by Sir Thomas Lawrence; gold rings that had belonged to the historian and traveller, A. W. Kinglake; a gold *stater* of Alexander the Great with Athena on the obverse and other relics associated with the Club. Other artistic possessions are locked away because of lack of space in which to exhibit them.

In 1929 an Artistic Committee was formed of Sir Reginald Bloomfield, R.A., Principal W. Rothenstein, Cecil A. Hunt, R.W.S., Mr. Mervyn O'Gorman, and the President of the Royal Academy, *ex officio*. Among its tasks specially mentioned was 'the acquisition of portraits and prints of distinguished Members, the Club collection of which is very inadequate'. There certainly was a good foundation for such a collection because many gifts of such prints and engravings had been received from the foundation of the Club onwards. In 1833 portraits and engravings were among the gifts acknowledged by the Committee. In 1835 Messrs. Colnaghi and Co., whose name is still very well known to all connoisseurs, then in Pall Mall East, were generous donors of portraits and engravings. In that year, also, Mr. Thomas McLean of the Haymarket presented the first

series of his royal folio *Portraits of Members of the Athenaeum Club*, a gift he followed up in 1836 by sending lithographic portraits of twenty-five other eminent Members, including those of Nassau Senior, Charles Lyell, Thomas Amyot, J. W. Croker, W. M. Praed and Isaac Disraeli. Thereafter, apart from the engravings presented by Sir George Richmond, R.A., already mentioned, there seems to have been a considerable interval before more were acquired, a lack of interest that is very evident if the disposal of Sir Thomas Lawrence's portrait of George IV was symptomatic of the general attitude of Members towards works of art. It was all the more surprising because from the start, artists had been favoured recruits and many were elected.

Much more concern with the artistic embellishment of the Club was manifest towards the end of the nineteenth century and earlier in the present century. Mention has already been made of the generous devotion of their time and energy by Sir L. Alma-Tadema and Sir E. J. Poynter who, together with Arthur Lucas, worked for three successive years after 1894 as a Decorations Sub-Committee, but not all the results of their labours have survived.

In 1898 the Committee recorded a valuable gift of forty proof engravings of portraits by Henry T. Wells of the Members of Grillion's Club. Herbert Herkomer, R.A., whose style like that of most of his English contemporaries is no longer fashionable, presented some of his etchings and prints in 1900. Then Arthur Lucas gave a delightful statuette of Minerva that survives in its glass case to catch many an appreciative eye. Before the Artistic Committee had been established there had been an appeal for such donations. Mr. John Murray added to the benefactions that he and his family more than any other publisher had bestowed upon the Club by presenting twenty-nine engraved portraits of original and early Members of the Athenaeum. The portrait of Herbert Spencer painted by Miss Grant, one that he preferred to Herkomer's canvas, was given to the Club by Miss Meinertzhagen in 1915. Other relics of that doughty Victorian, who worked hard for the Athenaeum, came into the Club's custody when the Herbert Spencer Trust was wound up. As they included diaries and letters which one or two scholars have wanted to inspect in the revival of interest in Herbert Spencer in recent years, the Club has handed them over to the University of London Library. Four or five years before the Artistic Committee began its work, wall space was prominently pre-empted in the Hall and corridors to house portraits of Sir Humphry Davy, Charles Darwin, T. H. Huxley, H. R. Tedder, Michael Faraday, Croker and Matthew Arnold. Those of Darwin and Huxley were the work of another famous Member, the Hon. John Collier, R.A., who became Huxley's son-in-law. A bust of George

Finlay the historian of Greece by J. Kossos (1837) was also presented in 1925.

In 1930 'several important additions to the artistic treasures of the Club' were listed as a result of labours of the Artistic Committee whose activities continued in subsequent years. They were thanked for their 'admirable work' in supervising the furnishing and decoration of the new Ladies' Annexe in 1936. In that year Max Beerbohm gave his drawing of the Rt. Hon. Stanley Baldwin to the Club. More engraved portraits, some of Athenaeum Members, were presented by Mrs. Freyberg in 1938. A notable addition in that year was a water-colour of Teignmouth by Turner, the gift of T. Cannon Brookes, Esq., who began a tradition of generosity to the Club loyally maintained by his sons. In 1946 the Ladies' Annexe, then reopened after the war, benefited by an attractive marble bust, presented by Mr. Hector Bolitho, of young Queen Victoria by W. C. Marshall, R.A., who was responsible for the 'Agriculture' group of statuary on the Albert Memorial in Kensington Gardens. More portraits, prints and drawings of former Members were acknowledged in 1947 together with portraits of King Edward VII and Queen Alexandra by Sir Luke Fildes, autographed by their Majesties.

As for the exterior decoration of the Club, Sir Alexander Gibb's generous offer to pay to gild Athena's statue over the entrance was greatly appreciated, although at the time Members and public alike were unaware of the identity of their benefactor: that Members alone were not the sole beneficiaries was evident in the extensive comment on the event in *The Times* of 12 March 1951 in which a classical scholar well-versed in ancient mysteries, noticing that the goddess was 'swathed in unsightly tarpaulins from head to foot', speculated upon the possibility that the Athenaeum was undergoing 'the annual purification of the Plynteria' but ruled that out on astronomical grounds in favour of the more likely explanation that Athena 'was changing her clothes, an anonymous Member having taken upon himself the duty, or privilege of a new dress, not perhaps too soon for she has had no such treat since the Club was founded . . . a perfect example of λειτουργία and not less pious than magnificent, for we know that the robe offered to Athena had to be of surpassing magnificence'. So since 1951 the 'goddess excellently bright' shines in London. She had much earlier attracted comment. In a long forgotten farce by a Second Empire critic and playwright, J. B. Planche (1808–57) there was the following dialogue:

Minerva – And there's the Athenaeum – my statue crowns the portico so wide.
Mercury – Let's hope the wisdom is not all outside.

The goddess might have been believed to have already arranged such a desirable state of affairs.

When the Rev. F. G. Waugh referred to Athena 'holding out her prone hand as if welcoming worshippers', it is evident that her spear has been added since the end of the nineteenth century. From the Drawing-Room window, an observant Member recently perceived that her 'prone hand' was not grasping the spear. Should she not lose it? A keen Hellenist met the challenge by pointing out that the Athenaeum's statue was modelled on the Promachos Athena, originally posed at Sunium where the crest of her helmet and the tip of her spear were said by Pausanias to have been a landfall for sailors in the Saronic Gulf, making for Athens. Certainly, the majority of remaining statues of the goddess, including fragments, show her with a grasping right hand. Early prints of the Club show her without a spear.

Particularly remarkable are the gifts presented by ladies, who cannot of course be listed as Members, usually but not always commemorating a husband, or other relative, or friend. Thus in 1966 Mrs. Winslow gave the Club two pictures by Charles S. Ricketts, R.A., in memory of Robert de la Condamine. In 1970 Miss Helen Barlow presented a portrait of her brother, the late Sir Alan Barlow, G.C.B., a Life Member (elected in 1915) and a Trustee. In that year also were displayed portraits fortunately depicted from the life of those other pillars of the Club, Sir Alan Burns, Lord Hurcomb and Mr. M. T. Tudsbery. Their likenesses had been commissioned by fellow Members, the first time, it is believed that gratitude for long years of assiduous service to the best interests of the Club had ever been so satisfactorily demonstrated. In 1965 some of his fellow Members had fittingly commemorated the memory of Iolo Williams in a way that perceptive man would have appreciated, by subscribing for two small watercolours by David Cox.

Such a sample list from a long record of generosity to the Club might be very considerably extended but the gifts cited above will fortify the view expressed elsewhere in this work that the loyalty and affection evinced towards the Club as an institution are indicative of a strength of sentiment of no common order.

Exhibitions

A pleasant feature of the Library is the series of exhibitions periodically changed. The Athenaeum has few pictures and little wall-space for them, so these attractive displays are a source of constantly renewed interest. In 1968, for example, a series of exhibits planned by Mr. Guy Hamilton relating to the many professions represented in the Club membership was inaugurated by the late Dr. W. S. C. Copeman, a generous benefactor. He arranged an exhibition of eminent members of the Medical profession who had early been Members of the Athenaeum, borrowing material from the Royal College of Physicians. This exhibition was followed by others on the Army and on Science. When Sir Thomas Monnington lent works by Presidents of the Royal Academy, Sir Charles Wheeler presented the Club with his marble statue of Aphrodite, which had been one of those exhibits. The French Ambassador, an Honorary Member, helped to arrange a striking exhibition of the works of French Impressionists which was later succeeded by another art exhibition which owed much to the help of the Ambassador of the Netherlands. A collection of letters, documents and notebooks which had belonged to Parson Woodeforde and his family was lent by Mr. Oliver Woodeforde on the occasion of a Lambeth Conference. A Christmas show was based on the works of Lewis Carroll. Some of John Gould's famous bird books made another colourful exhibition. In 1972 some of the Club's cartoons by Max Beerbohm (elected under Rule II in 1929) were on view. Such exhibitions can also make considerable demands upon the energies of the Librarian and her lady assistants.

Exhibitions in other rooms than the Library and Drawing-Room have also been a pleasant feature in recent years. In 1971–2 Mr. Henry Baker arranged an impressive exhibition of architectural drawings and plans made by his father, Sir Herbert Baker, the eminent architect (1862–1946), also a former Member of the Athenaeum. It illustrated some of his grand buildings in India and South Africa that many Members of the Club would not have seen. This exhibition was followed by a series of large-scale photographs of magnificent baroque churches and monasteries in Bohemia lent by Dr. Peter Cannon-Brookes.

Value of the Library

Referring in glowing terms to the Drawing-Room as 'one of the finest rooms in London' and to some of the other features of the Club, Mr. Ralph Nevill in 1911 said, 'But the chief glory of the Athenaeum is its library . . . it is by far the finest and most important club library in the world'. Saying that 'the annual expenditure on books since 1848 has averaged about £450, Mr. Nevill extolled the rare volumes, the books on history, topography, archaeology, art, and notably the pamphlet collection. Several hundred volumes contain pamphlets collected by Gibbon, Sir James Mackintosh, Morton Pitt, James Nasmith and others. From these now rare ephemeral publications much can be gleaned to illuminate political, economic, religious and social history of the last two hundred years. According to H. R. Tedder it was Henry Hallam who deserves the credit for forming this fine collection.

No Member of the Athenaeum needs to be assured about the value of access to a good library or to be reminded of all the many words written in praise of books. If Wordsworth was over-optimistic in regarding the 'substantial world of books' as 'both pure and good', he was not wrong in regarding a worthy collection of the kind of book that he had in mind as something 'around which our pastime and our happiness will grow'. Generations of men, of whom many were eminent in the annals of British cultural life, have been attracted to the Athenaeum by the knowledge that when they were elected, they would have access to a well-stocked library. If Samuel Butler had been a Member, he could have included the Athenaeum along with the British Museum and Mudie's as the places where, he said, 'he kept his books'. Even those Members who do not frequently have occasion to disturb the shelves probably agree with Sydney Smith that 'no furniture is as charming as books'. It is not only from books that Members in the Athenaeum can glean knowledge, for, as Samuel Johnson said, 'Knowledge is of two kinds. We know a subject ourselves, or we know where we can find information upon it.' Many Members who come to the Club Library in search of information, consult the Librarian who often has to act as a research assistant. In this task she can be assisted by other Members who may know the answer to the query or indicate where the answer may be found. A specimen list of some of the questions asked in a recent year included the following:

The influence of Cluny on the development of Romanesque art and architecture.

The date and further information on the erection of the Foundling Hospital, Naples.

Information regarding the foundation, character and Members of 'The Other Club'.

Particulars of the house in which Karl Marx lived in Clerkenwell.

Did Marguerite de Valois ever enter a convent?

Information on St. Ninian and Fastidius (*circa* A.D. 300).

Where can the discourse on the Copley Medal handed to the widow of Captain James Cook in 1776 be found?

Designs for stable clocks.

Information and illustrations on dinosaurs.

Anything about Marshal Zhukov.

The Jockey Society: a nineteenth-century establishment. What was it, and what did it do?

The history of the blacksmith and his craft.

Illustrations of the habit of an Ursuline nun in Paris in the seventeenth century.

Details of modern treatment of BCG vaccination for Tuberculosis.

Who painted 'Boats at Sainte Marie'?

Information on Sumer and the Sumerian Language.

A Questions Book is also placed in the Drawing-Room in which problems posed by Members stimulate others to provide answers. Biographical details of past Members (particularly original Members) of the Club, are constantly requested.

On a lower plane, the more philistine may be assured that the present cash value of the books in the Library – so rapidly have book values advanced – must now exceed that of all the other assets of the Club put together: the building, the furniture, the investment pool of stocks and shares, and the wine and spirits in the cellars. Nobody probably ever anticipated such a result because the books were never bought as an investment but for their intrinsic, their true worth. 'Sophisters, economists and calculators' therefore can appreciate the need to preserve intact so valuable a heritage, while even in their eyes wisdom can, after all, be justified of her children.

CHAPTER FIVE

The Athenaeum and Gastronomy

It must be admitted that some of the material advantages offered by the Athenaeum did not always meet with the same smiling approval as that which Prosper Mérimée bestowed upon his dinner in 1837. From early days in the Club's history some Members began using the blank space on the back of their bills to make comments upon the food and drink they consumed and the service they received. That some attention was paid to their remarks is indicated by the existence in the Club's archives of several small black-cloth volumes in which the bills so endorsed were bound. From the recurrence of the same complaints, it would seem that they had not always provoked the desired improvements. There were, of course, one or two constant grousers, periodically disgruntled by the food, drink, delays and cost of service. Alike for the glimpse these comments allow of nineteenth-century Clubmen at table, the sort of food they ate, and to some extent, of their character, these old manuscripts deserve a passing glance.

Taking a few at random, there was Mr. James Stuart who had to be content with mutton chops and a pint of sherry on 29 October 1832. He did not say that the chops were poor but begged 'to suggest that there should be now a joint daily at Five O'Clock as I know that it would be a convenience to the Members of ye Club as well as myself who are in the habit of dining at that hour'. He does not seem to have succeeded because he made the same observation on 31 October in the following year. If the joints were edible, other dishes often were not. The Rt. Hon. H. Ellis said on 10 April 1833, 'I was very hungry, had the appetite & I suppose the taste of an Esquimaux, or I could not have eaten the breast of veal'. Even potatoes failed to please. Nassau Senior, the economist, 'got only 1½ potatoes at ¼ before four, and those horribly bad'. There are rarely any indications of the replies received by the indignant Members, but here was one indication that the annual British potato harvest had been very defective. It would not then have been supplemented, as it would be today, by increased imports. In March 1836 Sir J. Stratton found his beef steak 'execrable, without a morsel of fat, altho' the Cook was cautioned'. His marrowbone, moreover, 'did not contain half a teaspoonful of marrow'.

Many of the complaints were about delays in the service. Mr. John Cowell on 26 August 1834 wrote a little time-table of his meal which was a dozen oysters. After forty minutes, which he declared that the waiter said was only thirty minutes, they still had not arrived. After fifty-five minutes, or forty-five by the waiter's chronology, he was eventually served. Apparently they had been worth waiting for because he just had room to write, in a scholarly hand, that 'The delay was accidental – admonished to be more careful in future'. At least he got a dozen oysters, a dish that his successor bearing that name would be very glad to get today when they seem to be priced off the Club's menu; no longer the 'poor man's food' memorably celebrated by Mr. Samuel Weller.

A keen determination to get value for money characterised many Members. In the 1830s Professor Sedgwick demurred at a charge of 1s. 6d. for a plate of cold beef. It is rare to find a Member complaining that he was given too much to eat. It was probably on grounds of economy that Professor Richard Owen found, on 28 February 1859 that his 'mutton pudding, in regard to its richness, seems to be too large', adding that 'a smaller size at 1s. 6d. would, the writer believes, be preferred'. A stickler for economy, Professor Owen had already pointed out, in a four-page note in December 1858 'written at ¼ past 4' that 'Members of the Club holding salaried offices which tie them to their duties until 4 O'Clock may feel, like himself, that the Club fails to afford to scientific men of moderate income, the comforts of a Club at moderate cost when resorting to it for luncheon when engaged to a late dinner, as long as the price of a plate of soup is doubled after four O'Clock'. His bill for Julienne Soup was 6d. to which Table Money of the same amount was added, but in those far-off days that entitled a Member to bread and beer as well. When the Club said that a brace of ducks cost 3s. 6d., it seems unreasonable for a Member to complain that 4s. for them cooked and served was 'too much', although one may envy his ability to have despatched them together with a dish of green peas on 18 June 1836, which in those days would not have come out of a tin or a deep freeze, after a plate of whitebait to the accompaniment of brandy and a pint of claret.

On 12 January 1836 Mr. C. J. Villiers who often adorned the back of his bills with acid comments, paid 1s. for two mutton chops, 6d. for rice pudding and extras, unspecified, 6d. Brandy was also 6d. He made no comment about the chops, but complained that he waited half an hour for the rice pudding 'and it was not half done when brought. It was said to be ready when ordered.' 'Stale whiting,' said another Member on 14 January 1836, apparently unconsoled by his two mutton chops, scalloped oysters and turnips that followed, fortified by a pint of stout and half a pint of port and a liqueur, all for six shillings and sixpence. Two other gentlemen dining together in the same month thought five shillings for their leg of lamb and spinach 'very exorbitant'. Members now need to re-calculate every year the present gold equivalent of the five shillings of 1836. 'Three shillings for a Turkey's leg', snorted another. In those days even the Club cellar was not immune from heavy criticism – 'bad Port', 'Sherry very bad', 'Beer invariably bad and sometimes not drinkable'. This would have been the 'table beer' that stood on dining and luncheon tables as jugs of water do today, its cost being part of the Table Money charged to cover the supply also of bread and condiments. In some nineteenth-century Clubs, cheese was also included, so impecunious Members could stave off hunger merely by paying Table Money. The quality of the beer supplied varied very much. In these days of mass-produced, nationally advertised and distributed drink, there is no memory of the great diversity available when hundreds of small breweries all over the country supplied local needs. Then, for example, Trinity College brewed the Audit Ale that Macaulay brought from Cambridge to Albany, and Clubs brewed their own. 'Small beer, my dear Father,' wrote Hastings Russell in 1844 to Lord William Russell, 'is one of the few things that Mammon cannot command in the Metropolis – it is not to be had for money, or love, in London can scarce procure it. There is one chance – the Clubs! *They* brew small beer. I could get some from the Guards were I in London. In general Clubs will send nothing out. But surely if Brooks's paid Sheridan's debts they will never refuse table beer to a Russell? Try Brooks's or any other Club.' (*Lord William Russell and his Wife 1815–1846* by Georgina Blakiston, Murray, 1972, p. 488.) At the Athenaeum a mixture known as 'Bishop's Hat' is still obtainable, compounded from bottled Guinness, barley wine and bitter.

Complaints about coffee have continued down the centuries. Three Members added their signature on 6 November 1835 to a declaration, 'coffee very bad, so acid as not to be drinkable'. In March 1836 three other Members 'begged to submit that the price of a glass of liqueur (Curaçao) ought not to be a shilling'. All the prices here quoted were, of course, based on a gold standard, so they must be multiplied many times if they are to mean anything today.

Not all the comments were unpleasant. Mr. James Talbot who found his spinach 'abominably dressed' on 9 April 1836, and not, he said, for the first time, had the grace to acknowledge on 21 April 1836 that 'the spinach was well dressed'. Some of the most gratifying comments came from Members who had arranged convivial parties to which they invited other Members. Such dinners would presumably have been ordered in advance, giving the cooks sufficient time to go to some trouble in their efforts to please. Colonel William Macgregor, after a dinner for ten Members in 1837 at a cost of 17s. 6d. a head, reported that 'it was an excellent dinner'. More than half the cost arose from two bottles of champagne, one of hock, one and a half of Madeira, three bottles of sherry, one of port and five of claret. Shortly afterwards Sir Roderick Murchison with a bill for nine Members found the dinner 'remarkably well dressed and well served'.

But it was not necessary to organise a large party in order to get satisfaction. 'Dinner very well dressed', said Mr. W. J. Broderip in January 1837, and his table companion, the renowned Theodore Hook purred, 'so nice'. Between them they drank no more than a pint of Lisbon, a bottle of port and a shillingsworth of gin. Dr. Thomas Mayo dined on 25 August 1838 off calf's head with a pint of Madeira to his complete satisfaction; 'extremely well cooked Calf's Head', he said. 'Very good soup' was the opinion of Mr. Colquhoun in October 1838 after a shillingsworth of hare soup and a fried eel. Despite the declining credit balance in the Club's accounts in the 1860s some Members were gratified by the wine and food purveyed. Mr. Edward Porter and his five companions had no complaints; 'Dinner and Wine excellent,' was their verdict. 'We were much pleased with our dinner,' wrote Sir R. W. E. Forster after he and three friends had dined in February 1861 on whiting, côtelettes de mouton, filet de bœuf, widgeon, brussels sprouts and an omelette soufflée.

It is impossible, and probably always will be, to draw up a balance sheet listing complaints as debits and praise as credits. Consequently later verdicts on Athenaeum food much of which, it must be owned, was poor, may be quite unrepresentative of the general opinion of Members and their guests.

'Where is the Club-man to dine?' asked G. W. E. Russell in his entertaining sketches of the characteristics of forty-five types of people in Edwardian England. 'This is a vital question before he chooses his evening club. To reply first by negatives, he will not dine at the Athenaeum where all the arts and sciences are understood except gastronomy.'

That was in the days when it was said of a future Duke of Devonshire that 'Lord Hartington has only eight clubs'; so competition among Club chefs might have been expected to stimulate efforts to excel. It has never been a field in which the Athenaeum has either striven for or been accorded high honours. 'Intellect rather than love of comfort formerly distinguished most members of the Club,' said Ralph Nevill in his book on London Clubs in 1911, a somewhat strange backward glance at a time when almost all the first recipients of the Order of Merit were Members of the Club, 'and for this reason, perhaps, the Athenaeum has never been noted for its cooking. "Asiatic Sundays" was the name given to the Sabbaths, on which curry and rice always appeared on the bill of fare. Another Athenaeum dinner was known for its marrow bones and jam roly-poly puddings. Sir Edwin Landseer once denounced an Athenaeum beefsteak in a terse manner. "They say there's nothing like leather; this beefsteak is!" '

Other Clubs during the nineteenth century took greater trouble to provide good fare, but that was a new development. Neither White's nor Brooks's rose to very high standards according to Gronow who recorded an incident at Carlton House when the Prince Regent asked some of his friends from those elegant establishments at dinner one night what they had to eat there. They lamented one perpetual round of 'the eternal joints or beefsteaks, boiled fowl with oyster sauce and apple tart and very monotonous it is'. At once the Prince had summoned his chef, Wattier, who there and then agreed that he would be ready to organise a Club. Wattier's became for a while a highly fashionable resort at which His Royal Highness was often seen. But it did not last ten years. The food was exquisite but the gambling was ruinous.

Alexis Soyer, the famous French chef, author of *Gastronomic Regeneration*, made the Reform Club famous. He aided Barry in designing the kitchen there, but even so it is incredible that any kitchen could provide his stupendous banquets, with their bewildering variety of sixteen soups, sixteen fish, eighty-four dishes of poultry, game and meat, seventy sweets and desserts, all at one such feast, the like of which would be a sensation anywhere today. Crockford's in its heyday was renowned throughout Europe for the dinners cooked by another Frenchman, Louis Eustache Ude, and his successor Francatelli who later went to the Reform Club. But the Members of the Reform Club were on record in 1904 that the Union Club provided better food than they had in Pall Mall. There was certainly no stint at the Union Club where each Member consumed on the average about a pound and a half of meat at the ordinary dinner. If the Athenaeum refused to compete against such talent it was probably less because of its concentration upon the life of the mind than on account of the reluctance of most Members to spend money in or on the Club; an attitude which was a constantly limiting factor, frustrating the possibility of many improvements throughout the nineteenth century. A later commentator rashly and incorrectly made the Bishops the culprits. Mentioning the Athenaeum in his informative and excellently illustrated account of *White's 1693–1950* Mr. Percy Colson said

> 'the food there has never been particularly good – perhaps owing to episcopal influence on the committee, and during the late war it was unspeakable. I lunched there in 1940 and after a revolting meal my host said: 'Let's

> have a liqueur with our coffee to take away the taste of the food.' (The coffee incidentally had no recognizable taste.) We asked for Grand Marnier, Kümmel, Cointreau, Benedictine – they had all disappeared, probably down the throats of the Bishops. Finally we managed to obtain a very inferior cooking brandy. Even in mid-Victorian days the club was known for its indifferent food. It is said that Francatelli, the French Ambassador's chef, when told that his Excellency was going to dine at the Athenaeum, exclaimed: 'Ah! I shall never see my poor master again.'

If Athenaeum food was to be judged by wartime standards, the verdict could hardly be favourable. Rationing was severe and strictly obeyed. Eggs, butter, cream, meat, fish, fresh fruit and vegetables were no longer to be had in anything like sufficient quantities to supply the daily needs of London Clubs. Chefs had to do the best they could with commodities not seen in the Club before or since; whale-meat, snoek, frozen codfish; tinned processed meat-products; powdered potatoes, eggs, milk, and all the other substitutes that enabled beleagured Britain to survive. On Tuesdays, Wednesdays and Thursdays no wines were allowed with meals, while not more than one glass of sherry before a meal or one glass of port afterwards consoled Members for their enforced abstinence. There was however no such limit upon beer and spirits. As for the implication that sinister episcopal austerity had deliberately lowered gastronomic standards, it will be sufficient to say that it is rare to find more than one London Bishop on the Club's Committee, which more often has to manage without such guidance.

There is even less likelihood that any Bishop would be found on the Club's Kitchen Committee but that is not to say that their presence there would be otherwise than helpful. Mr. Colson cannot have it both ways. If the good taste of the Bishops had been responsible for the disappearance of the choicer contents of the Athenaeum cellars, their alleged influence on the Club's Committee is unlikely to have been as sinister as he suggested.

Some Members believe that the association of the Athenaeum with indifferent fare is by now one of those myths or stereotyped clichés, like its supposed domination by Bishops. Both are so well established in popular journalism and general gossip that they will never be given up, however excellent its daily bill of fare may become or however few its Bishops.

Sometimes also the charm of novelty lends enchantment to the food in another man's Club that his host does not understand. If Athenaeum meals were indifferent, it was not for lack of interest by the Club Committee. A light luncheon buffet had been started in the Upper Smoking Room which was claimed as a success in the Annual Report of 1926. Then also guests were admitted to tea in the Coffee-Room, as they already had been for lunch there. In 1931 the Committee reported that they 'had constantly in view the necessity of establishing a high standard of quality and cooking'. After the war years, when all standards were drastically reduced and when almost double the peace-time number of meals was called for, new efforts were made to hasten recovery. In 1950 the Committee recorded their gratitude to the well-known catering firm of Lyons for reviewing the Club's resources without charge and suggesting various improvements which had been made as the result of their advice. That much more was needed might be the first supposition to occur to anyone who learns that, apart from temporary halts in 1949, 1957 and 1958, the number of meals served in the Club from 1946 onwards decreased every year; the fall being from 70,904 in 1946 to 30,727 in 1970. As though perturbed by this startling decline, the Committee again appealed to Messrs Lyons for advice in 1966. As a result the kitchen was somewhat improved. It was then thirty years old and declared to be on the verge of collapse. Still the decline continued. In 1970 the Kitchen Committee that had been allowed to lapse was again constituted. With a new Steward in 1969 some Members may have hoped for a fresh start and perhaps a change from Club dinners of warmed-up left-overs from lunch, but the Steward contracted a fatal illness, dying relatively young in 1972.

Aware that few more than a small band of stalwarts usually dined at the Club, a critic may assume that the majority of Members were of Samuel Johnson's opinion that 'he who does not mind his belly will hardly mind anything else', and so went elsewhere. A longer historical perspective puts the matter in a different light. Between 1940 and 1950 the number of meals served at the Athenaeum was abnormally high. Although, in comparison, the 30,727 meals served in 1970 seems alarmingly low, it is nevertheless necessary to go back to 1890 to find a year between 1870 and 1917 in which as many as 30,727 meals, the figure for 1970, were served. A severe crisis in national affairs such as the two world wars seems to draw men together more often in their Clubs.

This interpretation is slightly complicated by the fact that in 1914, a few months before the outbreak of war, a majority of Members was at last found to agree that a beginning should be made with the admission of guests. In putting that question to the Annual General Meeting the Club Committee said that they felt that 'in view of the changing tendencies of Club life, the time has come when, in the interests of the Athenaeum, the question of the introduction of strangers to dine in the Coffee-Room should again be considered. The proposal was introduced on two occasions (1892 and 1902) by individual Members, and in 1908 by the Committee: it was defeated each time, but by successively decreasing majorities.' Accepted today as a matter of course, and for lunch and tea as well, the extent to which it did indeed point to 'the changing tendencies of Club life' is not easy now to realise. These 'changing tendencies' as well as the admission of 'strangers' were not noticed in Mr. Humphry Ward's *History of the Athenaeum*, an omission that reveals the expectation in the minds of two elderly gentlemen, Tedder and Ward, in the heyday of the reign of George V, of a recovery from the post-war economic difficulties. 'Recovery' would mean a return to the life that Members of the Athenaeum had known before 1914. Some social habits had already changed then, although they apparently called for little comment. One that can be fairly precisely dated from the records of the Athenaeum was the decreasing popularity of dining at a Club and the growing preference for lunching there instead. It occurred between 1880 and 1881 when for the first time more Members lunched than dined. Thereafter the trend was unmistakable as the following table indicates:

Number of Members participating and average price per meal

	1880		1881		1911		1913	
	Number	*Price*	*Number*	*Price*	*Number*	*Price*	*Number*	*Price*
Meals served								
Breakfast	5,154	1s. 5½d.	5,151	1s. 5½d.	2,102	1s. 5d.	1,499	no prices reported
Lunch	15,113	10½d.	15,584	1s. 0½d.	18,520	1s. 3d.	14,459	
Dinner	15,329	3s. 4¾d.	15,530	3s. 4¾d.	7,678	3s. 8d.	4,844	
Supper	126	1s. 0½d.	85	1s. 0½d.	25	1s. 2d.	22	
	35,722	1s. 8¾d.	36,350	1s. 8¾d.	28,325	1s. 10½d.	20,824	

As other Clubs reported a similar trend it is evident that one of those changes was taking place in social habits for which it is as difficult to account as it would be to say why many young men whose hair would have been uniformly cut short before 1939 began to prefer to appear unshaven and untrimmed after 1960, or why young ladies all wore skirts before 1914 although many now appear in trousers. Such matters seem to baffle even ingenious minds who adduce sunspots, the internal dimensions of the pyramids of Egypt, the prophecies of Mother Skipton or the positions of the constellations as matters full of immense significance for the human race holding the clue to the strangest vicissitudes in its puzzling history.

With the admission of guests to the Coffee-Room for dinner, the number of dinners served steadily rose after 1915; but so did the numbers of lunches to which guests were not admitted. During the First World War many more Members made a habit of eating at the Club; in 1915 the total number of meals served was 27,320; in 1919 it was 35,761. Thereafter, except for 1923, the total again began to fall although it rose to 33,622 in 1926 as a result of a lengthy visit from Members of the United Service Club, 'the Senior'. With the institution of dinner discussions in November 1926, the creation of bedrooms for Members in 1928, the admission of guests to lunch in the small Guest Room made available during the extensive alterations in 1928, more meals were served as the following comparison shows.

	1926	1928
Breakfast	1,343	2,739
Lunch	19,836	23,982
Dinner	8,377	9,406
Total	29,556	36,127

By 1932, after which the Committee ceased for some years to report such details, the total had risen to 41,637. The desperate crisis of the Second World War drew many more Members to the Club, just as had happened after 1914. So great was the influx that the Coffee-Room became very crowded at lunchtime. No guests were allowed there except on Saturdays and Sundays but they had to be entertained in the small room now used for light lunches. Even there Members were limited to one guest at lunch and two at dinner in the Coffee-Room.

Awareness of the declining popularity of Club dinners may have made it easier to win assent to the innovation that allowed Members to have guests at dinner, just as it aided the inclusion of women among such guests after June 1972. After all, most Members never dine in the Club. Those who did so were remarkably consistent in their expenditure. Between 1887 and 1911 the average amount spent on the four meals that it was possible to consume in the Club hardly varied. Only once was it as low as 1s. 9d. (1897), and only once was it as high as 2s. 3d. (1891). For ten years the average cost was uniformly 1s. 11d.; for seven years it was 2s. Throughout those twenty-four years two shillings may be taken as the average, so that a Member eating breakfast, lunch, dinner and supper, with tea and coffee, was able to do so for eight shillings a day. Such strange uniformity does not seem to indicate acute dissatisfaction with the Club's menus or distaste for the products of its chefs.

Such minor details record facts not readily found elsewhere. Connoisseurs and those interested in the wine trade may wish that more details had been preserved about changes in taste among Club Members, such, for example, as that revealed by the Club House and Finance Committee's somewhat rueful reference to the marked decline in the consumption of 'Spanish and similar wines which yielded the greatest relative receipts'. Sherry, Port, Madeira and Marsala fell off from a previous average of about 338 dozen to 278 dozen, or 18 per cent in a few years before 1872. This brief reference to wine may serve as a reminder that evidence of dissatisfaction with Club meals did not latterly extend to complaints about the wine served, recalling the naval stoker's remark that there is no bad beer, but some beer is better than others. It calls for a tribute to the enduring vigilance and skill of successive Wine Committees in which Members and their guests will willingly join.

Such a tribute is the more necessary because histories of Clubs do not usually have much to say about wine, which matters less because memories of vanished vintages and long-forgotten wine lists can be merely tantalising irrelevancies to those with no hope of profiting from either. That many Members of the Athenaeum can recall Cockburn's '27 port and other splendid wines is small consolation to them or anyone else now that stocks are exhausted. Nevertheless there are always hopes that something as good may yet recur to exert those beneficent powers celebrated on many occasions by the Laureate of the Sublime Society of Beef Steaks whose spirit undoubtedly awoke fellow-feeling among many of the Founder Members of the Athenaeum. He it was who declared:

Yes! wine is a charming eye-water,
It brightens the organs of sight;
Makes an old woman look like her daughter,
And sets a bent cripple upright.
It clears the thick brain of the muddy,
It tears off hypocrisy's veil;
It mellows the glow of the ruddy,
And flushes with beauty the pale.

With me it's a magic reflector,
I catch a new life from its beams;
Spring up a fresh youthful projector,
And build up a world of new schemes.
I'm no more an old heavy pacer,
To creep through this valley of care;
But a light-footed hard flying racer
That scampers through moonshine and air.

The Duke of Wellington's Funeral Procession in Pall Mall.

The Drawing Room, painted by James Holland in 1830

Two reasons there are for our quaffing;
  One, Sorrow's keen sense to subdue;
One, to quicken gay jesting and laughing,
  And bring pleasant follies in view;
That's the play that I wish not to banish,
  The picture I trace with delight;
I sip that its charm may not vanish
  Ere Time block the scene from my sight.

(from verses by Captain Charles Morris
in the posthumous *Lyra Urbanica*)

Cooking, like all other arts, finds competent executants more easily than highly talented performers, while the upper levels are more rarely attained and then are not always maintained, not even in renowned establishments. Food, moreover, is far more closely related to general health in the minds of many today than it ever could have been in the days before the discovery of vitamins and the essential contribution of trace-elements in nutrition. No Club is a pioneer in this respect, not even the Athenaeum, where traditional fare still preponderates as it does elsewhere, to make a food-reformer's nightmare of all Clubs and almost all restaurants. Not material satisfactions alone therefore enable the Athenaeum to attract and retain Members; indeed the Athenaeum has survived despite its reputation for neglecting to provide them.

CHAPTER SIX

The Club's Staff

Histories of Clubs and Institutions rarely have much to say about the staff who maintain the whole life and activity of the building. Occasional references appear to their long hours of work, to the cost of feeding them, and, in the Athenaeum at least, yet more occasional references to the discharge of one or two of them in the nineteenth century for drunkenness after due warnings had been ignored, or for other bad behaviour. When such details are noticed, they are rarely, if ever, presented in their context, which is the social and economic state of the country and contemporary opinion. This is unfortunate, because the history of the Clubs of the nineteenth century furnishes one or two grim illustrations of the foresight of the Rev. Thomas R. Malthus (later a Member of the Club), who, in 1798 warned that the rapid increase in population would 'subject the lower classes of society to distress and prevent any great permanent amelioration of their condition'.

In the middle of the nineteenth century, the Union Club in Trafalgar Square, maintaining the charitable tradition of the medieval monasteries, was sending every day the residues of broken bread, meat, bones, dried, used tea-leaves and coffee grounds, to relieve the destitute of the parish of St. Martin-in-the-Fields. In 1851, the year of the Great Exhibition of ingenuity and progress, 2,919 lb of bread, 3,389 lb of meat, 1,540 pints of dried tea-leaves and 1,394 lb of coffee grounds were so provided, all being thankfully received. Those were the days when a 4-lb loaf cost as much as about seven old pence, a leg of beef was 3½d. per lb, mutton or veal about 8d.; days when a Crimean veteran who had lost a leg in the war was engaged by that Club 'as "Sweeper of the Crossing" with the usual allowance of 3s. per week on trial, should the Secretary upon enquiring find that his character is satisfactory'. Complaints about mud in the 1830s had resulted in a reduction to 2s. a week. Sometimes payment was refused. Similar sweepers were employed by the Athenaeum and 'the Senior', such was the muddy and filthy state of Trafalgar Square and Pall Mall in the days of horse-drawn traffic, and before wooden blocks replaced the cobble-stones in 1879 when the Athenaeum contributed £105 towards the cost. It was in this environment that Sydney Smith, when told that similar wooden blocks might perhaps surround St. Paul's Cathedral, observed that the Dean and Canons need only lay their heads together and the job would be done. He was himself a Canon Residentiary after 1831.

None among the 'toiling masses' today has any experience or any idea of the hard life to which gross and mounting over-population condemned their predecessors, as Malthus had correctly forecast that it would. Competition for any employment, particularly less skilled work, was intense, so inevitably wages were low. Hood's pathetic 'Song of the Shirt' reflected the misery over-population had brought, particularly upon unfortunate women and girls. There were always many applicants for any employment. When Queen Victoria ascended the throne in 1837 a man waiter at a West End Club would expect £30 a year, a head waiter £40, a chief cook £150, and the steward £200. They would have had free food. Hours of work were prolonged. At the Union Club the Hall Porter was on duty from 7.30 a.m. till 9.30 p.m. On two days of the week he was allowed half an hour off duty and Sundays off every other week.

In 1860 when the Union Club advertised their vacancy for a Secretary they received 413 applications. Clubs did not owe their existence to such a pool of cheap labour because they existed before it had become vast, and they survive now that it has disappeared. They made a small contribution to its relief.

Some Members thought that the Athenaeum ought to do more for the poor than paying rates and taxes and making an annual contribution of ten guineas to hospitals. In May 1865 the Annual General Meeting was invited by the Earl of Caernarvon and the Bishop of Oxford, his seconder, to accept a Motion that the Club should present the Rector of St. James's, Piccadilly, 'annually not exceeding 50L. to be applied by him towards the Parochial Charities or any of them, excluding those of a religious character'. When this Motion was put to the Meeting it was rejected by 116 votes to 92. It was but one Motion among others, such as the Committee's own proposal to raise the annual subscription from six to seven guineas, which also failed. Neither proposition would be expected to provoke comment from non-Members; but feelings had been aroused which were further stirred by a long article on the question in *The Times* on 19 May 1865, in which the attitude of the Members of the Athenaeum towards the poor was used to illustrate some shrewd observations upon changes then becoming apparent in English social life. For that reason quite as much for the comments upon the Athenaeum, the incident merits attention.

In the 1860s, which was the decade of Matthew Arnold's celebrated onslaught in the *Cornhill Magazine* on the cultural poverty of his contemporaries from the

Court and the aristocracy down to the miserable denizens of London's fetid slums, *The Times* pointed to the way in which 'the hard rational dominion of "sophisters, economists and calculators" was drying up the wellspring of human charity' and greatly weakening the traditional society that had been 'entirely constructed upon a system of personal relations in which individual feelings of loyalty and obedience and affection held communities and nations together in warm though uncertain relationship.' 'Society and the science of politics is becoming a mere question of the balance of interests, to be determined simply by calculations of utility.' Country gentlemen were being transformed. The English merchant was being replaced by 'Firms, Companies and Associations which are just alike all the world over, and which remain the same machines though every person who first started them should be dead'. They were

> impersonal entities with limited liability. Charity, from being the personal act of the charitable, is becoming hardened into Funds, Institutions and Societies. Nowhere perhaps, is the change more remarkable than in Clubs. In the last century from the Clubs of the *Spectator* down to the Pickwick Club, they were little individual societies, with quaint personal humours about them. Now they are vast impersonal masses; a sort of congealed interest . . . with little sign of any feeling about them. . . . A Club . . . what is it often nowadays but a machine for providing the Members with a certain amount of comfort and luxury? What is its Committee but a mere set of 'economists and calculators' whose sole object is to provide the greatest comfort for the least money? What is the income of the Club but a mere fund for eating and drinking, reading newspapers, playing billiards, smoking and like occupations? We are not writing without a text (the article continued) nor framing a general indictment without distinct evidence. The Athenaeum, one of the most distinguished great Clubs of the West End of London, has just rejected by a sufficient decisive majority, a proposal to subscribe £50 a year to the non-religious charities of St. James's Parish. One only of the fifteen Clubhouses on the best sites in the parish, the Carlton, subscribed to any charitable purpose.

The remainder 'disavow any claim, beyond the rates and taxes they are legally compelled to pay'.

A lively correspondence resulted in which the Rev. John Edward Kempe, then Rector of St. James's rebutted two arguments; one, that a subscription list for voluntary gifts was the right solution (which he declared had already proved a 'mockery and a delusion'); and another that a Club would have to change its Rules in order to subscribe or face the Court of Chancery on a charge of illegally disbursing Club funds. Much heat was generated by the clash of opinions. Lord Lyttleton felt so strongly in favour of the Earl of Caernarvon's Motion that he lithographed a circular supporting it and when the Motion was lost he told *The Times*, 'This question will not be allowed to drop', making light of suggestion that a reversal of the Club's decision would expose the Committee and the Club to an injunction by which the Court of Chancery would forbid any such grant. He was quickly told that any lawyer could soon convince him that he was mistaken. All the arguments for and against the proposal were examined in an article in the *Pall Mall Gazette* on 26 May 1865 in which the issues were summarised as

(1) Are the Members of the Club in their corporate capacity under a moral obligation to subscribe to the charities of the Parish?
(2) If they are, can the Annual Meeting make a rule that a subscription shall be paid?
(3) Is the subscription useful?
(4) Can the Club afford the money?

Dismissing (3) as too wide a question, and (4) as 'impertinent', the article concentrated on the first two points. Various considerations were adduced to support the conclusion that Clubs should be absolved from any moral obligation to subscribe. It declared 'that every one is morally bound to subscribe to the charities patronized by the clergy of the parish in which he happens to live is a monstrous proposition. . . . The private subscription list is clearly the true course.' It was sufficient, the writer thought, to answer that 'the concerns of the Club are simply the "comfort and luxury of its Members", to use Lord Lyttleton's phrase, and such moral obligations as arise immediately out of the promotion of that object. Their moral obligation as men, the Members never meant to delegate.'

Two other periodicals entered the fray. The *Saturday Review* supported the charitable aim of the noble Lords and their allies but the *Globe* took the same line as the *Pall Mall Gazette* in a more objectionable manner by sneering at Lord Lyttleton for 'fouling his own Club-nest'. In explanation of this unpleasant charge, the *Globe* made the more plausible objection that 'the matter is not one for public agitation at all; and that to make it such cannot be deemed, at all events, exactly a legitimate proceeding, when adopted on the part of Members of the Club themselves.'

Because it was typically the attitude of most Victorians, including very warm-hearted, reflective individuals such as Macaulay, the words of 'A non-subscribing sort of fellow' contributed to *The Times* on 20 May 1865 are worth quoting. He wrote as 'a sexagenarian who remembers Pall Mall clubless', and

> upon the one solid ground, that the direct tendency of the proposal is to promote improvidence and weaken self-reliance – the mainstay, the prop, the sole abiding hope of the poor. Hardly any class of skilled mechanics earn higher wages than the first-class journeymen who work for the Members of Clubs, or are more able to lay by for a rainy day. By insuring them against want when that day comes, you simply abolish the natural and most effective check on idleness and excess.

It was not that the 'non-subscribing sort of fellow' was eager to shut the gates of mercy on mankind. He was not against charity as such.

> If we are to subscribe, let it be for hospitals, or houses of refuge, or ragged schools – for anything and everything, rather than run the remotest chance of encouraging tailors and shoemakers to get drunk. I honour the benevolence of Lord Lyttleton and Mr. Kempe. It is their political economy I doubt; and it is political economy, after all, that must decide whether any particular form of charity is good or bad.

John Ruskin at that time was attacking with special virulence what he thought to be the exaggerated reliance upon 'political economy' in *Unto This Last* (1862), *Sesame and Lilies* (1865), *Ethics of the Dust* (1866) and later books. He had been recruited to the Athenaeum under Rule II in 1849, so he may have been among the substantial minority who thought that the morals of tailors and shoemakers in the Parish of St. James's might survive the ministrations of their Rector in dispensing the Parish charities. The spirit prevalent in the Athenaeum at that time denied him the opportunity to display his skill at the expense of its Members. The Club was in the middle of an acute financial crisis. The effort to raise the subscription by one guinea a year had failed, a fact that another Member did not hesitate to publish in a letter to *The Times* as an additional argument against the proposed charitable gesture. The plea failed.

Not until fairly recent times has every Annual Report of the Athenaeum Committee concluded with a grateful acknowledgement of the devoted service rendered by the Club's staff. Nevertheless it was not unrecognised to some extent during the nineteenth century. In contrast with the more generous attitude taken in recent times, long service was then rewarded with a pension on retirement somewhat exceptionally, and that was long before the Old Age Pensions scheme had rescued thousands of aged men and women from the

Workhouse with its almost prison-like harsh rules and its separation of man and wife. Secretaries of the Club were much better treated, so was Spencer Hall the Librarian on his retirement in 1875 after forty-two years' splendid service. He was made an Honorary Member of the Club without having to pay an entrance fee or an annual subscription. Similar privileges were extended to the Secretary of the Club Mr. J. C. Webster, who retired in 1897 on a pension of £400 a year, although Humphrey Ward hints, perhaps out of compliment to Tedder, his successor, that he was not very efficient. No Secretary could, however, have made the financial diehards budge. It was a task that had defeated the Committee itself. Those were the days in which George Moore, arriving in London in quest of literary fame could set himself up in comfort in Jermyn Street, employ a valet, and live as a young man about town on one sovereign a day. But he, however, like two other famous Irishmen, Oscar Wilde and George Bernard Shaw, was not a Member of the Athenaeum.

In the nineteenth century and earlier, the general run of humanity were expected to work up to the end of their lives. Hobbs, the Athenaeum's Butler, retired after forty-seven years' service in 1896 on a pension of £80 a year, but he did not live long. Webster fortunately survived to enjoy his pension and his membership until October 1908. His successor Henry Richard Tedder, already Librarian, was yet more liberally rewarded. His salary, originally £175 a year, rising to £250 a year, was increased; in 1901 he was given £700 a year, a handsome income by contemporary standards. In 1914, shortly before his death, Field-Marshal Earl Roberts, K.G., V.C., O.M., as Chairman and Trustee signed an appeal for a testimonial to Tedder who was later presented with a portrait of himself by C. Hall Neale and 'a handsome cheque' at a ceremony over which the Archbishop of Canterbury presided. This event commemorated Tedder's forty years' service. He was to continue for eight more years. He retired in 1922 on a pension of £600 a year with a gratuity of £200 and admission as a Member of the Club without entrance fee or subscription. A 'Head Smoking Room Waiter', a 'Woman Chef', a Hall Porter, all had small pensions in the 1880s.

Such payments were exceptional. In 1880 when John Bennett, House Steward, retired he was awarded a pension of £150 a year which was not ungenerous, but he had been with the Club since it began in 1824. He, like the Groom of Chambers, John Wagstaff, who was then also pensioned, did not live long to enjoy it. Until 1922 when Tedder retired, the Club never spent as much as £600 a year on pensions; for many years none was paid. After Webster's death in 1908 the total never reached £100 a year before 1923. From immemorial antiquity men were expected to provide for their own welfare and that of their family, if they had one. When too old to work or when sick or disabled, they became the charge of relations or of some charity.

When Lloyd George and Winston Churchill laid the first modest foundation of the Welfare State by their Old Age Pensions Act of 1909 they did no more than provide five shillings a week for those British subjects over seventy years of age whose total income was eight shillings a week or less. Their initiative was opposed by many 'social reformers' in the Charity Organisation Society and even by 'social theorists' such as Sidney and Beatrice Webb on the grounds that such general relief would sap individual initiative and lead to general demoralisation. So the Committee of the Athenaeum were not inconsiderate or harsh employers if judged by contemporary standards. They provided a settled livelihood, a livery, food and shelter in a dignified establishment in a period when such advantages were the summit of ambition of countless thousands. Throughout the nineteenth century the growth of population had been so accelerated that it outstripped the efforts being made to develop the productive resources of the country. Gross over-population had created a vast reserve of uncared-for children who grew up, if they survived, as many thousands did not, to compete, unskilled, semi-literate and often illiterate, for employment of any kind.

Nobody who has not personal memories of the slums of the large cities of the United Kingdom and Europe before the advent of the Welfare State can have any conception of the abject poverty in which hundreds of thousands then strove, in so far as they had strength to strive, for bare survival. This, the common fate of the masses in all over-populated countries since the dawn of history, seems to have been regarded as one of the facts of life beyond the power of individuals to remedy except perhaps to some extent by almsgiving. As for any action by the Government, central or local, beyond the very limited scope of the Elizabethan Poor Laws as they had been slightly amended in the eighteenth century and subsequently, it would have been opposed as the Old Age Pensions Act was opposed in the early twentieth century. Such was the prevalent state of opinion on poverty in the early nineteenth century; a time when three shillings a week was thought a sufficient contribution from a wealthy Club to the crossing sweeper outside their doors by men who might have paid sixty to eighty shillings at the Clarendon Hotel for the only genuine French dinner that it was possible to find in Regency London. Spurred by their reading of Marx and Engels, later demagogues with scant regard for historical actuality, have, for propaganda reasons, perverted history in their desire to nourish class hatreds. They have sought bogeymen who, because they organised and invented so as to employ others and grow wealthy themselves, may be deemed personally responsible for those dreadful miseries of past ages. But it was not only in overpopulated Britain that helpless mouths cried for bread and redemption from their harsh fate. After reviewing the autobiographies of twelve average nineteenth-century Americans, a writer in the *New Republic* (16 September 1972) reported, 'I can reach but one (unavoidable) idea myself: we are all very lucky not to have been born as an ordinary American in the nineteenth century.' For then, as he points out, 'an immense percentage of life had to be devoted to sheer work and drudgery'. Then, too, 'how infrequent and scant were any pleasures and how little opportunity there was for any life of the mind. All in all – except for the lucky few – existence was a hideously boring prison.'

With the vast progress of technology, means have been provided to allow the generous impulses common to the best of humanity far more scope. Today the attitude of mind of the Victorian era towards the poor seems singularly harsh, although of course it was then nothing new, because all the emphasis in earlier centuries, as then, was upon duty, not upon rights; except, it may be rejoined, upon the right to property. But among the best of the wealthy British, property also involved duties. Immense sums were devoted to charitable purposes to build schools, almshouses, village halls and churches. In almost every village there was a 'big house' to which the villagers could resort for advice and aid and from which the ladies would emerge on many a charitable errand. If private property was respected, so was the duty of self-help and self-improvement, by which, and by which alone, it was then supposed that property could be honourably acquired. Club servants like all other wage-earners, were expected to save money. When in 1885 the Committee decided to pay all salaries and wages monthly instead of quarterly, they said that the change would be 'a great boon to those concerned, especially in the lower grades of the servants, and it tends to encourage thrift'. It was a period in which 'my station and my duties' was a guide to conduct; very different therefore from later times in which 'he wants it, let him have it' has become an acceptable idea; times in which it now seems to be assumed by many that everyone has a 'right' to food, clothing, shelter and employment. Neither Club Committees nor the society from which they came would have regarded individual 'needs' in this way as equivalent to a valid claim upon society as a whole that legitimately demanded satisfaction.

Unless such considerations are borne in mind it may seem extraordinary that it was not until 1919 that the Club Committee declared for the first time in their Annual Report, then nearing its hundredth issue, that they 'were glad to recognise the assistance they have had from the staff under harrowing conditions'.

This acknowledgment came after four years of desperate warfare in which the patriotic immediate enlistment of all fit Club servants had been recorded, almost as something naturally expected. Some Members also joined their regiments, but as officers. During the Second World War the situation was very different. Members and staff were brought together by actively sharing common dangers on the roof as fire-watchers and in underground Air Raid Shelters. When everybody was 'in the ranks' day after day and night after night, they inevitably became more conscious of their common humanity. From its Interim Report to all Members of 18 November 1940 and in subsequent Reports the Athenaeum Committee always gratefully acknowledged the energy, the resource, the strenuous efforts, the loyalty and the devotion of the Club's staff.

During the nineteenth century, having provided, as they no doubt considered they had done, for the material needs of the Club's servants, the Committee did not neglect their spiritual welfare. On Sundays as many as possible assembled to march to church. In 1866 the Club Committee decided to pay a teacher recommended by the National Society promoting public education to hold a night school to impart elementary instruction to the Club's servants. Evidence of the efficacy of this laudable innovation has not survived. It followed an earlier initiative by the Club servants themselves according to a press cutting of 1843:

> A library was established at the Athenaeum in November 1841 among the servants of the Athenaeum Club and has been attended with all the beneficial effects anticipated. The project was sanctioned by the Committee who gave 5L towards the formation of it. The subscription is one halfpenny a week or sixpence a quarter – is voluntary, and confined to persons of the establishment: only three do not subscribe. The secretary has a *veto* on the choice of books. Works on party politics or polemical theology are not admitted.
>
> The work most in request is The BIBLE – a copy of which it might fairly have been assumed, was, in this age of cheap distribution, home and *foreign* in the possession of all persons of the class and character of servants; after this, Blair's Sermons and Nicholl's Help to Reading the Bible, then Scott's Novels and Poems. Cooper and Marryat's Novels and Burn's poems . . . it already comprises 126 volumes. The servants in bad weather stay in the house to read instead of going to public houses.
>
> Books were taken home and into the park in fine weather.
>
> Servants who could previously read very imperfectly, have applied themselves and now read with comparative facility.

This library has been maintained, and to it Mr. John Buchan, M.P., later Lord Tweedsmuir, presented some books in 1928.

When an independent investigator, who managed the Duke of Sutherland's establishment at Stafford House, was asked to inspect the Club's domestic arrangements in 1883, he praised the 'discipline, order, attention and contentment' of the Club servants. His commendation contrasted markedly with a Report by a Club Committee at that time denouncing waste and extravagance in the kitchen where 'the breakages were terrible'. In relation to the very different price-level today it is astonishing to read of the great concern caused in 1870 when the weekly cost of board for a Club servant rose from 7s. 10d. (39p) to 10s. 1d. (50½p).

After 1914 the fearful catastrophe of the First World War naturally bore heavily upon all Clubs, in common with the country at large and all national institutions. All the Athenaeum's servants of military age immediately offered to enlist in the Army. By 18 September 1914, six weeks after the declaration of war, ten were already with the forces. By March 1916 the total was twenty-five, two of whom had been killed. Three Members had by then also been killed. It was then that in addition to replacing the men servants with older men, waitresses also were employed for the first time. Some were retained, but men servants returned until the Second World War, after which nearly all the Dining-Room staff were women. It was not until some years after the Second World War that the last waiter retired.

Lady Assistant Librarians had already been engaged before 1924 and a succession of ladies became the Club's Librarian after the death in 1943 of Sir Stephen Gaselee, Librarian of the Foreign Office; a striking character and personality, who had been the Club's Honorary Librarian since 1935.

A small Staff Benevolent Fund was constituted as a source of financial first aid in 1924 and a contributory pension scheme to provide pensions at sixty began in 1931, the Club's contribution being £250 a year. By 1937 it had accumulated £2,237, so making further immediate allocations unnecessary. In 1936 the Club Committee recorded improvements in the accommodation and amenities provided for the staff as well as 'much improved' meals. They also observed that the arrangement concluded with the United Service Club in 1929 allowing the Athenaeum to close every other Sunday was 'a great boon to the staff'. This arrangement was interrupted by the Second World War, but resumed in 1949 until 1960, when both Clubs remained closed on Sundays. Tributes were paid in 1956 to some of the staff who had already a record of over twenty-five years' service. Such is the gratitude most Members feel to all the staff that it would be invidious to mention merely some of them. Many Members with memories reaching back over the years will however be glad to be reminded of the tribute then paid to Mr. C. W. Gedge, a former Wine Steward, whose genial presence had a vintage quality that seemed to improve the contents of all the bottles he dispensed. Mr. L. W. Middleton fortunately need not be praised in the past tense because there is not a Member who is not in his debt and none whom he does not know. His retirement at the end of 1973 after forty-seven years' service came as a shock to Members, not twenty of whom could remember the Club before he was appointed. On learning of his forthcoming retirement a Member living in Scotland who was elected in 1937, sent him a message through the Secretary, which may speak for all the rest. 'I should like you to tell him sometime how much I always appreciated his kindness to me from the very first day I became a Member. When I needed guidance or help as a very undistinguished new Member, Middleton would give me the advice I needed with superb tact and my difficulty, whatever it was, vanished as if it had never been.' Among his less pleasant activities was that of holding intruders at bay. There is a story of that eminent advocate, F. E. Smith, later Lord Birkenhead and Lord Chancellor, who began making a habit of entering the Club in order to visit the lavatory, although he was not a Member. On being challenged, he feigned surprise, saying, 'Oh! is it a Club as well?'

Any Club historian must sometimes wish that some at least of his task might be undertaken by one of the staff. Some of them have had to put up with a good deal from one or two of the Members, particularly in their later years. In the days before the Second World War, when page-boys were employed, one obeyed instructions to call a noble Member every afternoon as soon as his car had arrived after tea. He was always found to be asleep in a deep armchair, so the page-boy had to wake him.

'Your car is outside, my Lord.'

Partially roused with difficulty, His Lordship mumbled,

'My car, my car, what about my car?'

'It's outside, my Lord.'

'What's outside, boy?'

Relations between Members and the staff are kindly, as might be expected between people often meeting every day of the week. 'The Athenaeum' describes more than the Members, the building and its contents, for the staff are as much a part of it as anyone or anything else. Sometimes such a relationship has had a novel manifestation. Before the Second World War and the days of oil-fired boilers, an ex-Navy stoker was among the employees. One day he was hauled before the Magistrates on the extraordinary charge that he, being the worse for drink in Trafalgar Square, had mounted ladders lashed to Nelson's Column, put there for the exclusive use of steeplejacks, and had ascended to the top of the Column where he had danced a hornpipe in honour, presumably, of the hero of the Battle of Trafalgar. Stirred by such a daring feat, one or two Members of the Athenaeum went to the Court where they recovered their stoker, by then sober once more, by paying his fine.

CHAPTER SEVEN

Ladies and the Athenaeum

As the history of the Club records, its Founder, J. W. Croker, intended it for literary men and artists. Its first rule, he said, was that 'no one shall be eligible except Gentlemen' and they had to be distinguished in cultural life. In the social atmosphere of the first quarter of the nineteenth century, the idea that any London Club should admit ladies on equal terms with gentlemen, indeed on any terms, is unlikely to have occurred to anyone. Ladies had very occasionally been inside the Club on special days as guests. At first, before the Clubhouse was built, they had not been invited to the weekly Monday conversaziones, in the temporary rented premises, but that was no doubt because the purpose of these weekly meetings had been to make Members better acquainted with each other, and with the Club. As soon as the Club's success was assured, this attitude changed, as the following passage shows. It is from a letter sent on 26 February 1830 by Charles Lyell, later Sir Charles, to his sister (*Sir Charles Lyell, Bart. Life Letters and Journals*, 1881, Vol. I, p. 236):

> I wish you had been in town at the opening of our new Club, the Athenaeum, which is reckoned the most elegant turn-out of all, and for a fortnight gay soirées were given to ladies between nine and twelve o'clock, and it still continues to do so every Wednesday which I hear is to go on for months. It is really worth seeing and fitted up in a style which I must say would be ridiculous, except for receiving ladies. There has been a great deal of fun about it and verses innumerable. Some of our members grumble at the invasion, and retreated into the library, which was respected at first, but now the women fill it every Wednesday evening, as well as the newspaper room, and seem to examine every corner with something of the curiosity with which we should like to pry into a harem. They all say it is good for bachelors, and makes married men keep away from home, and talk of a ladies club, etc. As the house was much admired, the number of candidates increased prodigiously. The ballot, which in a smaller house was a nuisance is now an agreeable muster.

The Rev. Francis Waugh reported the lament of an unnamed misogynist of the same date: 'We are now really in our new palace, and we throw open its gates every Wednesday evening to whomsoever, among your gentler sex, are disposed to enter . . . I, who am a hermit in my own way, and by no means too inclined to sociality, must confess that I never felt a more melancholy pang than when, for the first time, I beheld, from the large chair in which I was "quietly inurned", a party of invading Amazons, with bare necks and yellow gowns, sweep across the chambers I had hoped would have been for ever sacred to frock coats and the modest virtue of cravats . . . true, that Wednesday is only one day in the week, but, then, that one day unsettles us for the six others . . . Besides, what mischief to the *tone* of our society! Instead of the learned silence hitherto breathing around, or the murmurs of scientific discussion or literary dispute, we hear the *suaves susurri* of "Last night – charming woman – beautiful eyes – good bust – pretty ankle!" ' These reunions were, however, highly appreciated by others.

Young Mr. T. B. Macaulay, devoted as he was to his sisters then living in Bloomsbury, does not seem to have escorted them to a Wednesday evening party at his new Club, although evidence is not lacking that he used to go there himself while he had chambers in Gray's Inn, between 1830 and 1834 when he left England for India. Contemporary evidence of the success of these evening gatherings is rare.

There has been some confusion about this development. Tedder in his article on the centenary of the Club in 1924 said that ladies had been invited to the Monday evening parties but Ward correctly said that they were not. Neither referred to the Wednesday evening parties held when the new Clubhouse opened.

There is no mention of these mixed parties in the Committee's Annual Report. They seem to have been continued in 1831 until 7 June when the Club Committee 'took into consideration the special summons this day "To consider the expediency of admitting ladies on the Wednesday evenings in June and a proposition that Ladies be admitted" was not agreed to.' No reasons were given for the decision to end these parties for ladies. No complaints were entered in the Club's records. They had been a remarkable pioneer effort that may well have been something of a social sensation, for no other Club is known to have been stimulated to copy them, neither did the idea to which Lyell refers, that ladies might have their own clubs, come to be realised until much later.

Ladies were generally supposed to dislike Clubs but not all wives resented their husband's absence at a Club. Sir Charles Lyell recalled a conversation on 6 January 1832 at the home of 'my favourite', Mrs. John Lockhart, Charlotte Sophia, Sir Walter Scott's eldest daughter, when 'Conversation Sharp' 'began to rail at clubs'. "Well," said Mrs. Lockhart, "I don't know what I should do

The Drawing Room today.

The Upper Smoking Room.

without the Athenaeum. Lockhart is never so entertaining as the days he looks in there, and that is five days a week, but I don't let him stay there long."'

Thomas Walker in 1835, in his praise of Clubs in general and of the Athenaeum in particular, was at pains to refute objections by proving that they had an elevating, civilising influence, far superior to that of 'taverns and coffee-houses'. Far from leading into bad habits, Clubs encouraged temperance, were economical and they saved men a great deal of time. He told the ladies that their influence was so beneficial that 'it is a natural step from the comforts of a Club to those of matrimony, and I certainly think that there cannot be a better security for the good behaviour of a husband than that he has been trained in one of these establishments'.

Ladies were not the only 'strangers' excluded from the Club because on 12 March 1833 the Committee revoked the resolution of 22 November 1825 whereby they had been entitled to bring one visitor each at the Monday evening meetings of Members. How long those parties continued is not evident from the Annual Reports which ceased to report their cost to the Club. Humphry Ward's *History* does not mention them but it does record the presence of 1,130 ladies and children in addition to 400 Members to view the Coronation procession of Queen Victoria (on 28 June 1838) and an almost equal number for the funeral of the Duke of Wellington on 13 November 1852. Unlike the United Service Club opposite, the Athenaeum arranged for no ballot for seats and made no charge, refreshments being provided at the Club's expense. That there was 'a good deal of over-crowding' seems a very mild description of a scene, the bare prospect of which would occasion terror today, if only for the reason that has always made the difficulty of admitting ladies seem to be insuperable, and that is the impossibility of providing adequate lavatory facilities in the limited space of the Club.

Much more recent experience fortifies this belief that it is almost incredible that the Club's resources were then able successfully to entertain the vast number of guests who crowded in to see the Coronation procession in 1838. When arrangements were made for viewing the Coronation Procession of King George VI and Queen Elizabeth in 1937, the Committee found that it had considerably over-estimated its resources in trying to accommodate and feed 933 persons. When Queen Elizabeth II was crowned in Westminster Abbey on 2 June 1953 plans were made to erect scaffolding as in 1937 but to provide no more than 542 stand-seats and 100 standing places. Twice as many applications for tickets were however received, so that they had to be allotted by ballot after applications for only one seat or one standing place had been granted. Three services of breakfast, lunch and tea were provided and some rooms had to be transformed for the benefit of ladies. In 1953 as in 1937 Mr. M. T. Tudsbery as the Club's honorary Consultant Engineer made himself responsible for all the intricate technicalities involved in the siting, planning and erection of stands as well as internal structural modifications to cope with the invasion. The success which crowned his efforts and those of the Club's gallant staff was measured by the gratitude of the visitors and their hosts; by the handsome contribution the sale of tickets made to the Club funds, and by contrast, the sight of unfortunate spectators herded into Waterloo Place wading through sewage as the drains became blocked in the temporary conveniences erected there by Public Authority. This experience within living memory must deepen amazement at the fortitude of our Victorian predecessors who somehow managed to cope with 600 more than the 930 found to be almost unmanageable with all the improved equipment of 1937, and more than double the number of those accommodated in 1953. It is the more surprising because no mention is to be found in the Minutes of the Club Committee in 1838 of either preparations for the event or an account of its difficulties. In the early nineteenth century there must have been a robust determination to make the most of any opportunity for unusual excitement. In his entertaining book *The Prince of Pleasure* J. B. Priestley describes scenes witnessed at Carlton House in June 1811 when the Prince Regent opened it for public inspection. On the third and last day thirty thousand people were said to have stormed the building. Such was the crush that 'ladies were to be seen all round the gardens, mostly without shoes or gowns and many almost completely undressed and their hair hanging down their shoulders'.

In considering the slow progress made in entertaining ladies, it must be remembered that men were also excluded unless they were Members. Until 1914, 'strangers', that is, men guests, could not be entertained at lunch or dinner. This was not because, following the Athenians of old, all non-Members were regarded as barbarians. Other Clubs had the same rule. Special dinners could however be arranged in honour of distinguished visitors as when Monckton Milnes, Lord Houghton, organised a dinner for Longfellow in June 1868.

By 1889 guests, men only, were admitted to the Travellers' Club next door 'because numbers were dwindling'. Repeated efforts at the United Service Club to allow men guests resulted in the grudging admission of ten only at dinner on any one evening in 1890. It was not until 1892 that they could be entertained also at breakfast and lunch. It must further be remembered that ladies were not seen in the very few restaurants then in London. Thomas Walker, in his revealing essays, *The Original*, said of London (on 9 September 1835): 'For the most part, female society is only to be met with at formal and laborious dinners, and overcrowded and frivolous parties, attendance on the latter of which men of sense soon find out to be a nuisance and a degradation.'

Before the First World War had shattered the ordered social round of Victorian and Edwardian England, a London Club was regarded as a haven guaranteeing dignified seclusion and repose, away from the toil and troubles of the world. It was, according to an observant Bishop, a place 'where women ceased from troubling, and the weary were at rest'. In this vein George Augustus Sala went further by describing a Club as 'a weapon used by savages to keep white women at a distance'. Even then some bold spirits elsewhere flouted convention. In 1867 a daring Member of the grand Union Club in Trafalgar Square, actually brought two ladies into the Strangers' Room where he regaled them with biscuits and wine. In the previous year the necessary majority of two-thirds which had not been secured when the proposals had been made ten years previously, had voted to allow Members of the Union Club 'to receive their friends at dinner in the Room known as the Strangers' Room', but nobody could have imagined that the 'friends' would be ladies. However the Club Committee decided 'not to interfere in such a matter unless the introduction of the fair sex became a matter of such frequency as to inconvenience Members'. Apparently the incident was not repeated, for nothing further is recorded about ladies at the Union Club until the German Emperor Wilhelm II paid a State visit to London in 1891, when Members were allowed to bring two ladies to lunch; but that was an isolated event.

After the First World War, in which women were much more actively involved than they had ever been in previous conflicts, many of them found new and more varied opportunities in social, economic and cultural life. As more and more of them began to undertake business and professional work that had hitherto been done by men, it no longer seemed reasonable to assume as a matter of course that they should never be seen in restaurants or inside a man's Club, as guests. At last in 1921 the United Service Club, familiarly known as 'The Senior', converted some of the rooms that had been added when the Club was extended in Pall Mall (1910) into reception rooms and a dining-room for lady guests. Long desired by many Members who had always been able to show ladies round the Club at stated times, the proposal to provide them with any refreshment was always defeated. Naval officers in particular were the most outspoken against the proposal; one old Admiral blurted out at a General Meeting, 'For God's sake don't let them in here. It's the only place where I can get away from my family.'

After 1921 Members of the Athenaeum had, therefore, been able, during their annual month's visit to 'The Senior' to discover the merits of an attractive suite of rooms for ladies. However much some of them may have wished that they could enjoy similar facilities, no way of satisfying them seemed open. There was no possibility of enlarging the building which is smaller than 'The Senior'. If more space could have been secured, it was needed for more bedrooms (not provided until 1928) for Members and resident staff.

At last, in 1935, an opportunity occurred to acquire the lease of a splendid large house, No. 7 Carlton Gardens, not far from the Club. Despite the Committee's recommendation, the proposal was not approved by the Annual General Meeting, although the need for additional accommodation was growing. In the following year the lease of a similar house, next door to No. 7, No. 6 Carlton Gardens became available. An Extraordinary General Meeting was summoned to give the Committee authority to proceed. In the notice convening the Meeting, the Committee set out the following reasons in favour of their proposal.

1. The number of guests who are being entertained in the present building is increasing and there are complaints from Members of consequent inconvenience.
2. A considerable number of Members desire to entertain lady guests.
3. The number of Members' bedrooms is inadequate to the demand.
4. The sleeping accommodation for female servants is not in accordance with modern regulations.
5. The Library has outgrown the space which the existing building can provide.

Although the Committee stated that these reasons had not been placed in order of importance, the sequence of No. 3 after No. 2 startled many Members whose lively imagination led them to fear that the document before them would inevitably and immediately suggest a use for a Ladies' Annexe quite inconsistent with the character generally attributed to the Athenaeum. It must be assumed that the Members attending the Extraordinary General Meeting of 26 March 1936, in approving the Committee's proposals were not swayed by the unintentionally provocative recital of some of the advantages they could expect to enjoy at No. 6 Carlton Gardens.

This splendid late Georgian house, once the London home of Gladstone, was then rented from the Crown Estate Commissioners, as it had been built on part of Crown land, the site of the garden of Carlton House. It provided five reception rooms, four Members' bedrooms, ten maid-servants' bedrooms to accommodate twenty maids. Its spacious dining-room on the ground floor and large, comfortable drawing-room on the first floor afforded good accommodation but were occasionally overtaxed.

Attractive as the new facilities for entertaining ladies were, the new Annexe ultimately became an increasingly heavy burden on the Club finances. During the Second World War it was closed, but expectations that it would be reopened after 1944 were for some time disappointed because of staffing difficulties. When these were eventually overcome there were high hopes that the Ladies' Annexe would be increasingly used with the resumption of more normal social life, as the devastation caused by the war was gradually repaired. Many ladies were brought there as guests. Members could buy books of tickets enabling any lady whose name they wrote on them to go there alone or with friends at tea-time. Nevertheless it soon became evident that the use made of the Annexe was declining. Despite special appeals by the Chairman of the Club to all Members, in 1950 and again in 1952, to make more use of the Annexe, the number of meals served there steadily declined. In 1951 about 9,000 lunches and 8,000 dinners were served. By 1960 the demand had fallen to 5,515 lunches and 5,113 dinners, figures showing that on the average a Member of the Club only took a lady to the Annexe about twice a year, or that half the membership did not enter its doors from one year's end to another. Despite the offer made by some Members to contribute financially to ensure the continuation of the Annexe, an offer that enabled the Committee to keep it open throughout 1959, it was evident that such generosity could not compensate for the growing liability of an Annexe already costing the Club £6,000 a year. In that year the matter was decided for the Club by the Crown Estate Commissioners who refused to renew the lease when it expired in 1961.

When it became clear that the Ladies' Annexe at No. 6 Carlton Gardens would have to be closed, Mr. M. T. Tudsbery was asked in May 1959 to review all possibilities of finding alternative accommodation, by sharing an Annexe with another Club, for example, and to assess their technical and financial implications. It was in the light of his very thorough study that his plan to excavate the new Annexe was finally accepted, to be carried out under his expert supervision. Permission was sought in 1960 to excavate under the garden to provide new rooms there and to enlarge those already there, the Billiards Room and a room used by Club servants. Permission to build above ground had been refused by the Crown Estate Commissioners who however consented to the excavations. When the proposals were put by referendum to the Members of the Club there was a majority of seven to one in their favour. At the Annual

General Meeting of May 1960 it was reported that the Committee, after taking expert advice, had appointed Mr. Victor Heal, F.R.I.B.A., as architect for the work. To pay for the work, Members soon oversubscribed an issue of £45,000 redeemable notes of £100 each not bearing interest, the Club meeting the balance of the total cost of about £60,000. On 2 September 1961, No. 6 Carlton Gardens was closed, and the new Annexe made ready. Over the steps down to the entrance of the Annexe a fine Greek inscription, selected at the Committee's request by Mr. E. V. Rieu that well-known translator of Homer, proclaims 'But follow me within so that I may offer you hospitality'. Calypso's lady-like language to Odysseus has sometimes been colloquially transformed to 'Come along with me and I'll stand you lunch' or, of course, tea, dinner or a drink. A passer-by was heard to explain it to a friend as 'the new synagogue'. Before the Annexe was opened there was an evening party at which the whole Club was thrown open to a limited number of lady guests on 27 September 1962.

This development elicited gratifying evidence of the loyalty and devotion many Members felt towards the Club. Already in 1962, among the record of gifts that are a regular feature of the Club's Annual Report, it was announced that Members, who wished to remain anonymous, had surrendered £700 of Redeemable Notes, an example followed by many others in later years, while Dr. W. S. C. Copeman had given £300 towards furnishing the new Annexe, a gift recorded on the glass panels of the balcony that were one result of his generosity. Mr. W. Reeve Wallace, a greatly respected Member, who was regularly to be seen in the Club to which he had been elected in 1910, presented six framed Piranesi prints not very long before his tragic death in a fire. They are now hanging in the gallery. A magnificent grandfather clock and other decorations were added as a result of a generous gift by Sir Eric Pridie. Whatever the attitude taken towards ladies by Club Members in the previous century, and however much the motives for acquiring a Ladies' Annexe in 1936 may have appeared to have been selfishly considerate of Club Members alone, there can be no doubt about their willingness to make considerable sacrifices on behalf of ladies or of the warm welcome reserved for them in our own times.

Nevertheless many Members and their ladies had cause to regret the disappearance of No. 6 Carlton Gardens. After standing derelict for some years, it and the similar house next door were destroyed in order that a commercial building in steel, glass and concrete on stilts could be built on their site.

To continue to be able to receive lady guests, Club Members had to sacrifice prized amenities. They lost their Billiards Room with its two large full-size billiard tables; they sold their complete but bulky set of bound volumes of *The*

Times, replacing them at a cost of more than three times the sum they realised by a microfilm copy. The new Annexe consisted of a comfortable lounge, dining-room, bookstore and bar, as well as cloakroom and lavatory accommodation which no ingenuity could contrive in the limited space of the main Clubhouse. Completely refurnished and with modern kitchen equipment, the new Ladies' Annexe, convenient as it is, inevitably lacks the space and elegance of Gladstone's house.

Members lost more than their Billiards Room and their original copies of *The Times*, because three-quarters of their long Upper Smoking Room was taken to provide staff bedrooms no longer available in Carlton Gardens. That room had been lined with bookcases housing nearly 8,000 volumes, and several hundred had also been housed on the shelves in the long Drawing-Room at No. 6 Carlton Gardens, so the Club was forced to sell thousands of books, many greatly missed by Members. Several card tables at which leisured and retired Members of the Club used to enjoy an afternoon game of whist and the newer game of bridge, which began to gain popularity after about 1903, were then banished to much reduced quarters in the small West Library.

In 1972 it was announced that the Club's Committee had decided, for an experimental period of twelve months, to admit lady guests to the Coffee-Room for dinner in the evening and to the Drawing-Room upstairs. There was not a murmur of objection to this arrangement at the Annual General Meeting, whatever the private feelings may have been of some who were aware of the nineteenth-century attitude to ladies in Gentlemen's Clubs. Those who feared a great invasion proved to have been mistaken, for very little use was made of the new facilities. Some Members believed that the greater comfort of the armchairs and sofas in the Annexe would be found to be a greater attraction to the ladies than the hard leather of the Drawing-Room after dinner, whatever interest they may have felt in seeing it after dining in the Members' large Coffee-Room.

CHAPTER EIGHT

Finance

As the brief summary of the Club's foundation and early years has indicated, no special difficulty was experienced in raising over £43,000 to build and equip a new Clubhouse in 1830. Along Pall Mall, Barry's grand home for the larger Reform Club cost nearly twice as much, £82,000, in 1841. Running expenses in the Athenaeum's new home were naturally heavier than they had been in the smaller, rented premises, as the following comparison of some of the main heads of expenditure shows:

12 Waterloo Place				*The New Clubhouse*			
1 January 1828 – 31 December 1828	£.	s.	d.	*1 January 1831 – 31 December 1831*	£.	s.	d.
House Rent	900.	–.	–	Ground Rent & Land Tax	360.	12.	–
				Insurance on £40,000	100.	–.	–
Insurance	9.	9.	–	Portrait of George IV	128.	10.	–
				Assessed Taxes	283.	7.	2
Servants				Servants			
Wages	694.	7.	4	Wages	1369.	1.	8
Provisions	439.	5.	–	Provisions	379.	6.	1
Liveries	151.	6.	3	Liveries	105.	19.	–
Tax	48.	8.	3				
				Poor & Police Rate	84.	9.	4
				Water Rate	32.	–.	–
				Paving & Sewer Rate	225.	–.	–
Fuel				Fuel			
Coals	228.	7.	6	Coals	417.	16.	–
Charcoal & Wood	171.	2.	8	Wood	30.	–.	–
Light				Light			
Lamp Oil & Wax	214.	2.	7	Lamp Oil & Wax	133.	18.	–
Tallow Chandler	36.	–.	9	Tallow Chandler	14.	3.	10
Gas	60.	–.	–	Gas	474.	17.	7

Washing House Linen	211. 7. 6	Washing House Linen	248. 4. –
		Newspapers, Magazines	
		English	315. 16. –
		Foreign	63. 5. 6
		Periodicals	185. 5. –
Stationery & Printing	489. 16. 6	Stationery & Printing	209. 16. –
		Wine	1684. 1. 3
Wine	562. 19. 1	Damage at the Riots	77. 19. –
Coffee	22. –. –	Coronation Expenses	141. 2. 6
Library	506. 11. –	Purchase of Books	462. 10. –
Monday Evening Party	58. 16. –	Binding	63. 5. 7

It will be seen that the accounts were not presented in exactly the same form from year to year. Later in the century they were shown in considerably more detail. From the above comparison it is evident that the Club incurred no expense for the Wednesday evening parties for ladies, and that the Monday parties for Members only had been a charge on the Club's Budget. Therefore the ladies' hosts then had to pay for their own refreshments as well, as they would naturally be expected to do for their guests.

It might be thought that the novelty and the privilege of enjoying the magnificence of so grand a Clubhouse for the modest sum of six guineas a year would have been so greatly relished that every Member would be astonished at his good fortune in being free to enter it. As for the cost of meals in it, they were not merely to be had more cheaply than elsewhere but they were served in surroundings incomparably more elegant than any hotel or tavern could provide. While the early nineteenth-century coaching inns were good, they were also expensive, but the smaller cheaper taverns were mostly poor or bad. There were few other public eating-places for men and none for ladies. Nevertheless it was not long before the services provided at the Athenaeum seemed to be taken for granted while any proposal to increase the annual subscription was always defeated. Matthew Arnold's castigation of his contemporaries for tolerating the fearful squalor of London by exhibiting the vice of decadent Imperial Rome of public poverty amid private wealth, *privatim opulentia, publice egestas*, comes to mind when reading about the fuss made whenever his fellow Members of the Athenaeum were asked to match their demands for comfort and service by providing more money.

In the 1850s Members complained about the cost of meals and poor cooking. They made a great row when the Committee endeavoured to make ends meet in 1854 by providing a chef to carve joints at lunch or dinner instead of allowing Members to hack off as much as they chose. Although the price of meat in the nineteenth century seems very low in comparison with the costs today, an average consumption of a pound and a half each at any one meal by Members was extravagant by our standards. Food prices then varied very considerably with the state of the domestic harvest and particularly of the available meat supplies, because those were the days before the iron steamship had superseded sail and before refrigeration had allowed vast imports of meat. In 1853 the Club had lost £1,000 on catering but still the Members defeated the proposal to stop them carving for themselves and to raise the price of meals. Some years elapsed before these very desirable changes were made. In 1861 a proposal to raise the subscription from six to seven guineas was defeated by one vote. Instead, the entrance fee was raised from twenty-five to thirty guineas and additional Members were elected. 'Let our debts be paid by future Members and not by ourselves,' was the principle on which they acted.

Until about 1855 no serious difficulty had been experienced in making ends meet. By that year the whole of the debt incurred by building and equipping the Club had been paid off; general repairs had twice been undertaken at a cost of £18,000; a surplus of £2,000 stood to the Club's credit and an average saving was being made, so it was thought, of £1,400 annually. Those hopes were not realised.

In 1865 the addition of a third storey, badly needed, was rejected because Members would not pay for it. They thus lost the chance of having it designed by Decimus Burton who, after forty years' service as the Club's architect, retired in 1864. To make the Club live within its means raised perennial difficulties, the more inexplicable because most, if not all the Members were well-off, and some were very rich. It is not possible to believe that the additional subscription of a guinea or two a year would have inconvenienced any of them. Many spent as much on a single dinner with a choice wine and brandy, and cigars.

A serious financial decline set in which was shortly described in a thorough review of the situation, the *Memorandum on Finance*, dated 28 March 1872: 'From and after the general repairs in 1856 the income has never again sufficed both to defray current expenses and to pay off the cost of repairs, so that the Club has never been free from debt at the end of the year. These changes reflect the changes in the times, more luxurious living, greater demands on the part of

Members and, combined with these, the notorious increase in the cost of living in London.' Few people are likely to be aware of the cost of upkeep and repairs of a building such as the Athenaeum's Clubhouse so it may be of interest to record that repairs and improvements had, by 1872, involved the following outlay:

1836	£8,059	
1845	£9,758	
1856	£7,822	
1865	£6,670	
1868/9	£4,181	(mainly the underground Smoking-Room and Billiards Room).
Total	£36,490	

Again the Committee pointed to the right solution, rejecting the practice of trying to raise money from the entrance fees of a flood of new Members. They referred to that and other expedients which they rejected, saying 'whatever scheme is adopted, it must be based on an increased income. No one who habitually frequents the Club can doubt that numbers [i.e. of Members] have reached the utmost limit consistent with comfort . . . an increase of the Annual Subscription of the whole Club . . . is the most simple, direct and effective – indeed the only one which would be sufficiently effective to accomplish its object.' In vain the Committee listed the subscription rates in a dozen of the principal clubs of London, many of whom charged eight guineas a year, while the Carlton, Junior Carlton, Reform and Travellers' Clubs demanded ten guineas a year. In the preceding year, 1871, the Committee had hoped to make the seven-guinea rate (adopted for five years in 1867) the permanent rate, but they were defeated by an Amendment which, although it renewed the seven-guinea rate, limited it again for the ensuing five years. So the crisis was prolonged.

To retain the additional guinea subscription levied in 1867 cost the Committee a hard struggle. By the time they had achieved that victory it was evident that another guinea was necessary, but the majority refused to pay it. Instead the mean device was adopted of requiring all Members elected after 1875 to pay eight guineas a year while the rate for the then existing Members remained unchanged. Herbert Spencer, Chairman of the Committee called upon to advise on finance reported in 1879 that this measure would in time 'more than suffice to clear off the whole debt and to produce the needful reserve fund'.

He was over-optimistic. Costs were still rising. At the end of every year the Club was in debt to its bankers, sometimes for over £10,000. Annually the general finances of the Club had to make good losses incurred in the Coffee-Room because the rise in the cost of provisions was not matched by increased bills. In 1884, when there were still 907 Members paying at the old subscription rate of seven guineas a year against 441 paying eight guineas, a motion to ask them all to contribute an extra guinea a year was 'urged most strongly' by the Committee. At the Annual General Meeting it was refused by an Amendment setting up a Special Committee, yet another, to enquire 'whether any, and if any, what reforms can be effected in the details of the expenditure'. The Rt. Hon. W. E. Gladstone would never yield to suggestions to join the Athenaeum because he preferred the United Universities Club, but his passionate zeal for the strictest economy that still flourishes in H.M. Treasury as an everlasting flower, desiccated and prickly, was evidently widely shared. Such had been the efficiency of the management of the Secretary and the General Committee and its Sub-Committees that the new Economy Committee had to report that it was unable to suggest any reforms. So once again the General Committee asked Members with what might be thought to be compelling reasons, to accept the sacrifice that one more guinea a year or rather less than fivepence a week, would inflict upon them. Although the great majority evidently did not have any strong views on the matter, because less than 100 Members out of 1,200 took the trouble to attend to vote on the day it had to be decided, the thirty-seven Members who were determined to pay no more carried the day under the two-thirds majority rule against the fifty-three who saw that the change was necessary. It was true that the floating debt was being reduced, as Herbert Spencer said it would be, as old Members died off and new Members paying eight guineas a year came to the rescue. In 1882 that debt had been £6,132. By 1885 it was £5,657.

In that year, however, 'foul smells in some public rooms' unavoidably drew attention to the dilapidated state of the old brick drains with their inadequate outfall, while other improvements were also necessary. At last the elements of economic management had been grasped by a sufficient number of Members to induce them to agree that they should all pay the same subscription of eight guineas a year, so the privileged majority faced an increase but not the minority who were already paying that amount. Before long this simple measure rescued the Athenaeum from its deplorable financial difficulties.

Those troubles were the more inexplicable because 1,673 candidates were waiting for election, therefore a mass resignation of Members dissatisfied by the demand for an additional guinea a year need not have perturbed the Club's

Committee. No candidate would have withdrawn because the subscription had been raised. But a rule made a two-thirds majority necessary before any such change could be made in the Club's arrangements, and it greatly delayed progress. Other Clubs experienced similar troubles, so that the idea that nineteenth-century Clubs were uniformly flourishing needs revision. A serious financial crisis rocked the Travellers' Club in 1857 and difficulties recurred there in 1872. The 'Senior' raised its subscription to £6 in 1854 and there were more troubles there in 1868 when the Committee's effort to increase the subscription again was defeated. Another defeat in the following year by one vote brought their resignation. General Sir Louis Jackson comments in his careful history of the *United Service Club* (1937), 'One is amazed at the pig-headedness of the minority of diehards who were enough to prevent a two-thirds majority, although it had been explained to them that the Club was moving towards insolvency; and that they would not be in the least inconvenienced by the measures suggested.' His words were just as applicable to the Athenaeum, and, indeed, to humanity at large, as Dr. Samuel Johnson observed about the great difficulty of raising rents in the Western Islands of Scotland, 'Those who have hitherto paid little, will not suddenly be persuaded to pay more, though they can afford it.' At last in 1884 the Athenaeum subscription was raised from seven to eight guineas. With the retirement of the then Secretary, and the appointment of his assistant who was also the Librarian, Mr. Henry Richard Tedder, as Secretary in 1889, a new era began in the management of the Club.

The improvement came none too soon because Members and the British in general were demanding more convenience and comfort in their lives. After 1886 when the Club decided to substitute electric lighting for gas it incurred a bill for £2,289 in the following year to pay for the cost of installing gas engines in the basement to drive the dynamos that were to provide the current. During 1886, the last full year on gas and lamps, expenditure was as follows:

	£	s.	d.
Lamp oil	105.	19.	–
Candles and wax	19.	4.	8
Gas	485.	18.	6
Lamps, gas fittings & sunburners	119.	12.	4
	£730.	14.	6d

Four years later the electric light plant alone ran away with £1,068 while £96. 2s. 2d. was still needed for lamp oil, candles, wax, gas and gas fittings.

In 1891 new dynamos had to be bought at a cost of £350. It was not until 1906 that the last entry for candles and matches occurred, £5. 13s. 1d. After September 1897 when the Club gave up generating electricity on the premises in favour of a supply from the St. James's and Pall Mall Electric Light Co., the cost of lighting fell considerably. By 1913 the bill amounted to £512. 9s. 11d. Electricity had undoubtedly fulfilled the promise of the Committee in 1886 that it would provide 'comfort for Members and the protection of books'.

There was now money to pay for such improvements. As the Committee recorded in its report of 4 March 1892, 'for thirty-five years preceding 1890 there had been no balance at all' yet, 'there was at the end of 1890 a net cash balance of £1,072, while in 1891, after paying heavy outlays of £2,256 on Extraordinary Expenditure, the balance was £1,175 while £1,500 was put into the Lease Renewal Fund'. A cash balance of £1,757 in 1893 was 'the largest for forty years', yet in that year the periodical autumn repairs and repainting, required as a condition of the Lease by the Crown, had cost £1,674. Club Members probably never consider the high cost of maintaining their building and its equipment. Carpets wear out, and they are expensive when rooms and staircases as large as those in the Athenaeum have to be furnished. A new carpet in the Coffee-Room cost £106 in 1894, and £195 had been spent on a carpet for the grand staircase in 1891. Such costs may seem incredibly small today, but they were paid in golden sovereigns, not heavily depreciated paper money. Thirteen years after Barry had improved the drainage system a sanitary engineer reported that 'with one or two small exceptions, the whole of the drains are very defective'. Heavy cast-iron pipes were declared to be essential, with the result that the Club had to meet a bill for £1,028 in 1899. Several pages could be filled with detailed accounts of various improvements and changes that have over 150 years very considerably altered the interior arrangements of the building that Decimus Burton completed in 1830.

Externally also a change was at last made possible by the Club's greatly improved financial position. In 1900 an additional storey was added to the top of the building and furnished at a cost of £15,427 without the Club again having to borrow money. Proposals so to proceed had been rejected by Members at the Annual General Meeting in 1865, 1887 and in 1888. Strong objections were then expressed to the considerable alterations proposed in the internal structural arrangements of the Clubhouse; to the additional financial difficulties the Club would incur; to the proposed increase in the number of Members as an aid in paying for it, and to the closing of the Club for a long period. In 1898 the Club Committee, in depicting the many advantages to be anticipated from the additional accommodation, were able to assure Members that the evils feared in 1887 and 1888 could be avoided. So their proposals were approved and the first major addition to the Club had been achieved with other improvements. No plans were made to provide bedrooms for Members.

Nothing was heard of financial difficulties thereafter until the troubled period after 1918. As an example of his careful management, it may be noted that Tedder arranged in 1904 for the hall and grand staircase to be repainted 'by the Club', by hired labour, at a cost of £354. 12s. 9d. when the best competitive tender for the work was £785. 16s. Such economy was the more valuable because although prices of many commodities declined on the whole during the hard-working nineteenth century, other costs were continually rising. Public expenditure, despite the most strenuous efforts by Mr. Gladstone and his disciples, continually increased. Taxes and rates levied upon all possible individuals and institutions rose as the following comparison indicates.

Annual Rent and Rates paid by the Athenaeum

Local Authority	*Year*	*Rent to Crown*	*Rates (net)*	*Parochial Rates*
Metropolitan Board of Works	1856	£360	£1,730	£201
City of Westminster	1900	£1,800	£3,938	£1,128

Such increases were but a few among the rising costs of maintaining the Club.

During the twentieth century standards of comfort and convenience were constantly advancing; the fabric, furnishings and equipment were always needing repair or renewal, but these recurrent expenses were met within a budget that had financed not merely electric lighting and new carpets, but a new top storey, without serious strain.

After 1890 the Club's improved finances removed money worries. None but a very far-seeing Member would have been deeply disturbed about the state of the country or Europe, despite occasional crises and sporadic evidence of acute social discontent. Club life, solid, comfortable and stable seemed assured. Yet some signs of change might have disturbed any less complacent observer. Old Age Pensions provided in 1909 and National Health Insurance arranged in 1911, both strongly contested measures, were the forerunners of a veritable social revolution by which the whole fabric of social life was to be radically altered as visions of the outlines of a Welfare State were slowly taking more definite shape in political life.

In 1903, the year in which it was reported that since November 1902 'Members have been able to make use of the Post Office Telephone Service', there were still 1,358 candidates hoping for admission to the Club. Many of them would also have been candidates for other Clubs, after the practice of the time, but few would have been likely to withdraw their names if elected elsewhere first, because the prestige of the Athenaeum still stood high.

In 1902 about 150 Members attended a grand dinner at which the Rt. Hon. Arthur Balfour, M.P., in their name greeted twelve distinguished guests, the first holders of the newly instituted honour, the Order of Merit. Many of the twelve were already Members. In that year also over 700 Members and their guests witnessed from the Club windows, the balcony, and specially erected stands, the Coronation Procession of King Edward VII. Yet the number of candidates for admission was shrinking each year. By May 1914 it was 1,011; in the mid-nineteenth century it had been half as high again. Then came years of war and all the difficulties war occasioned.

Four months after the Allied victory, the Committee, surveying the Club's affairs, reported that much needed improvements called for better lavatory accommodation (its improvement had been described as an 'urgent necessity' in 1917); a larger Writing Room, a better passenger lift, more space for books, an improved library catalogue; overtaking four years' arrears of book-binding, restocking the depleted wine cellar, and more china, glass, cutlery and linen. All these needs had to be faced in a period of rising prices. 'A serious crisis has arisen in the financial affairs of the Club', said the Committee. There were then 693 candidates on the books, so survivors who had withdrawn their names because of the war were offered reinstatement; an action which did not arrest the downward trend. In social affairs, as in meteorology, the old adage 'long foretold, long last', seems to hold good. Before 1880 the number of Club Members dining at night steadily declined; both trends seemed persistent. Clubs were no longer exerting their former attraction.

To meet the rising costs, there was, for the first time, unanimous agreement in 1919 to an increase of the subscription from eight to ten guineas a year. Noting that few Members had resigned and that no candidates had withdrawn because of that increase, a subscription of twelve guineas was accepted in the following year to come into force on 1 January 1921. When the Club celebrated its centenary in 1924 with a conversazione to which Members were able to bring ladies, over 1,100 persons were present. New energies were then forthcoming to improve the Club's facilities with results, already recorded, in the additional top storey. If it was hoped that more candidates would be attracted to the Club by these improvements, these hopes were not realised. In 1929 the Committee reported that the matter was 'still of some concern'.

With the increased subscription of fifteen guineas a year to finance the cost of the extensive building and furnishing the new top storey, prosperity seemed assured. There were satisfactory surpluses in the Club's annual accounts until 1936 when a deficit of £519 occurred on account of the Ladies' Annexe, opened in Carlton Gardens on 28 September 1936. An almost equal deficit occurred in 1937 but a surplus was restored of £750 in the following year, the last full year of peace.

Expenses were then already being incurred for air-raid precautions and nearly twenty of the staff were being trained as air-raid wardens. Additional expenses were soon incurred in strengthening underground air-raid shelters, in providing two-tier bunks for the courageous band of fire-watchers, repairing broken glass as windows were shattered by bomb blast, and other damage. Only those who lived through the period realise how narrowly the Athanaeum escaped destruction. Only they remember the daily racket of pneumatic drills in basements as shelters were being constructed and roofs reinforced; they who paced in the rain or over frosted or snow-covered roof-tops wearing steel helmets and gas-masks; who snatched a few hours' sleep between raids on improvised bunks in tiers in ill-lit cellars, or those who, when not on duty, contrived to reach their offices from the suburbs after London had been pounded by air-raids, by making their way often by devious routes over heaps of rubble, avoiding ponds and swamps where water-pipes had been broken – or by stepping over burning gas pipes. None but those who shared these experiences can realise how much lay behind the brief statement in the first Annual Report after the end of the war that 'the Club remained open for the use of Members and their guests throughout the War'. Only two or three hundred yards away on the same side of Pall Mall, the magnificent Carlton Club had been destroyed. From the ruins a future Lord Chancellor carried his injured father, Lord Hailsham, on his shoulders, a feat which stirred Sir Winston Churchill's memories of 'pious Aeneas' whom Virgil depicted as rescuing his father in a like manner from the ruins of Troy.

In the light of the very different economic and social framework of British society after the Second World War it is easier to understand why Club life did not revert, as on the whole it had succeeded in reverting after the First World War within a relatively short time, to the settled prosperity it seemed to have enjoyed in the 1930s. Long-term trends had then advanced sufficiently to be unmistakable and they were not propitious. Above all, the curse of monetary inflation soon bedevilled cultural life in general and consequently, Club life also.

Clubs and Monetary Inflation

Merely on the financial side the effects of war and monetary inflation began a period of increasing difficulty for London Clubs. In 1920 the annual subscription at the Athenaeum which had remained at eight guineas since 1885 was raised to ten guineas. In the following year it became twelve guineas. Such an increase of 50 per cent barely compensated for the decline in the value of money. Inflation, as Macaulay showed in his graphic account of the drastic steps to combat monetary depreciation towards the close of the seventeenth century, is a grievous curse afflicting all classes of the community. Of that period he said:

> It may be doubted whether all the misery which had been inflicted on the English nation in a quarter of a century by bad Kings, bad Ministers, bad Parliaments and bad Judges was equal to the misery caused in a single year by bad crowns and bad shillings.

Today his verdict will not be contradicted. Although the English price-level after 1918 was never restored to the level at which it stood before 1914, monetary inflation was halted, but not before it and its remedies had inflicted grave losses on the nation's economy. That cost was merely one consequence of a ghastly war that all but wrecked European civilisation. After the Second World War similar colossal losses were masked by a renewed and steadily worsening depreciation of the currency. As a consequence the financial plight of all fixed income groups, private and institutional, including Clubs and learned societies, inevitably became extremely serious. All expenses rose; heat, light, rates, food, maintenance, postage, books, periodicals, and, in turn, salaries and wages also. A few figures illustrate the effect of inflation on the finances of the Athenaeum since the Second World War.

Year	*Total Expenditure*	*Of which salaries and wages accounted for*	*Income from subscriptions*
1944	£32,279	£11,809	£24,688
1950	£46,598	£21,585	£31,953
1960	£64,363	£34,216	£45,548
1971	£99,687	£63,254	£70,864

Thus in the twenty years, 1950–70, total expenditure more than doubled, salaries and wages trebled, while income from subscriptions also rose to more than double the 1950 figure. In 1948 the subscription had been increased by three guineas to eighteen guineas; it was again raised in 1952 by three guineas, again by five guineas in 1966, becoming £40 a year in 1969. From 1885 to 1920 it had remained stable at eight guineas a year. Great as the contrast is, the true picture would make it greater by taking account of all the minor amenities and luxuries in service and equipment that have been sacrificed in order to prevent the annual subscription rising to yet higher levels.

Inflation afflicts institutions such as Clubs and learned societies with special severity because of the reluctance, already noticed as a psychological peculiarity of Club Members in the nineteenth century, to contemplate any increase in their annual subscription and in the cost of their meals. Why that attitude should particularly damage Clubs while it seems to have no similarly disastrous consequences for restaurants, theatres, holiday resorts, travel agencies, services catering for leisure or luxury, remains a mystery. It is a species of irrationality to which a Club such as the Athenaeum, the 'mental' Club, as Theodore Hook described it, might be thought to be immune. Members who had been retired for some years and all those living upon fixed incomes have, of course, no alternative but to reduce their expenses as all costs rise. When they have to pay double and treble or more on travelling to the Club, on their meals, food, clothes and all incidental and household expenses, their Club subscription becomes a serious burden although it may be of minor significance to all those still earning who can qualify for steadily rising incomes. In 1973 these difficulties were recognised, when at the Annual General Meeting the annual subscription was raised to £60 with a graduated scale of reduction for older Members. Inflation is a swindle that can yield only temporary advantages so long as it can rob the defenceless. Disregarding such classes, as politicians long tended to do until the Government belatedly intervened to help them, and concentrating instead upon still active members of the Club, it was long ago clear that financial conservatism is their second nature. Because it was already evident before the days of confiscatory taxation, it cannot be regarded as evidence of the decline of Clubs as social institutions. Reluctance to pay in order to maintain standards nevertheless contributes to that decline, of which, in the last fifty years and more, other symptoms have become manifest.

In an effort to preserve their amenities when they, in common with learned societies and professional bodies, share the economic, social and cultural decline of which inflation is an index, several Clubs have joined forces. Then a Club building, with all its memories and associations, disappears, to be replaced, as 'cold Speculation barters out the soil', by an economically more profitable construction that does not possess and may be long in acquiring the subtle charm and allure of the old familiar, more spacious home, whatever its short-comings and technological backwardness may have been. Where the Club is fortunate in owning its freehold it can temporarily, at least, profit financially, perhaps greatly, because inflation, combined with the scarcity value of the site, had vastly increased the price likely to be paid for it. The Athenaeum does not own its site, so nothing, except recognition of the contribution that its building (which it does own) makes to the architectural amenities of London, and a realisation of the intangible values contributed by an association such as that housed within it, will prove able to

> reject the lore
> Of nicely-calculated less or more.

Unless values other than those of money ensure the rejection of that lore, not merely Clubs, but buildings on other favoured sites, such as Trafalgar Square, Bedford Square and Carlton House Terrace itself, would be liable to disappear.

If an Athenaeum Member of 1913 could return he might be perturbed by some changes; but if he noticed any decline in the standards of some of the equipment, facilities and service, he would be gratified by some compensating improvements. Those who have known the Club in the inter-war years could say the same. It is now much better illuminated at night, the oil-fired central-heating plant is cleaner, more efficient, flexible and trouble-free than the old solid-fuel boilers. It also costs less to run. Such details, however, are of less importance than the quality of the membership. Some would be irreplaceable in any period. Among the Members lost since 1939 were Sir Max Beerbohm, Sir William Bragg, Sir Cecil Carr, Richard Church, Sir Henry Dale, Sir Charles Darwin, Lord Dawson of Penn, Walter de la Mare, Dean Don, Sir Stephen Gaselee, Philip Guedalla, Lord Hailey, Sir Frank Heath, Sir William Holdsworth, Lord Horder, Aldous Huxley, Sir James Jeans, Hilary Jenkinson, Sir Philip Joubert, Archbishop Lord Lang, Lord Lee of Fareham, Sir Edwin Lutyens, John Mackail, Lord Macmillan, Stanley Morison, Gilbert Murray, Sir Charles Oman, Alfred Pollard, Lord Reith, S. C. Roberts, Sir William Rothenstein, Archbishop William Temple, Sir D'Arcy Thompson, George Macaulay Trevelyan, Sir Llewellyn Woodward, W. B. Yeats and Sir Alfred Zimmern. Many more names could be added that future generations will regard as notable additions to a roll of honour of which not only the Athenaeum but Great Britain can be proud. Among them would be Bertrand Russell, Earl Russell, whose career inside the Athenaeum reflected the vicissitudes to which he exposed himself outside it. Elected in 1909 in the usual way, his attitude to the law of matrimony as well as to the First World War so affronted patriotic Members of the Athenaeum that a Special Meeting of the General Committee of the Club was summoned on 18 July 1916 to expel him. Two years later he was imprisoned. In 1952 the General Committee, meeting on 18 February 1952, elected him without any application from him under Rule II, unaware, as far as it can be ascertained, that their predecessors had expelled the man they wished to honour and who, they hoped, would honour the Club by accepting membership, as he did.

Memories of such eminent Members insensibly endure to blend with other associations, evocative of sentiments rarely analysed or discussed that nevertheless give rise to a sense of satisfaction and gratitude so personal, so intimate, that an effort to find words to describe it is very rarely thought necessary and is yet more rarely attempted. Such emotions are out of place in an account of the financial fortunes of the Club. They can never be an item in a balance sheet because they have no assignable money-value, although they alone create a club and they alone can preserve it.

CHAPTER NINE

Winds of Change in Clubland

Inevitably the history of a Club, in common with all history, bears the stamp of the period in which it was written. Earlier in this book it was said that the centenary volume published in 1926 reflected an assumption that after the fearful disaster of the First World War, the British way of life was gradually resuming the mode of late Victorian and Edwardian times. No such easy assumption was evident in 1945, while in 1974 it would be impossible. Many of the facts to be found in that earlier survey and in the present enquiry are the same, yet they wear a different aspect. The absence of guests, the attitude of the Club management towards ladies and towards the Club's staff, for example, got scant reference when they were not ignored in 1926. It did not then seem necessary to speculate about the future of Club life in general or about the Athenaeum in particular. Today changes in economic, social, moral and cultural affairs have been far too drastic to allow the complacency of 1926 to survive. Speculation about future developments in such circumstances, however hazardous, cannot be evaded.

An anodyne, colourless forecast being obviously otiose, any positive views will be either predominantly pessimistic or optimistic. A pessimist in this context may be described as one who contrasts the worst features of contemporary life with the best of some imaginary future or of some possibly equally imaginary past. Optimism, as it has well been said, must go all the way with pessimism but beyond it; it cannot be vindicated merely by ignoring, evading or explaining away the grounds of pessimism. Ample grounds for that pessimism are all too patently obvious to all those, whether Members of the Athenaeum or not, who derive their political and social philosophy from the great Humanist tradition exemplified by such thinkers as Plato, Aristotle, Cicero, St. Thomas Aquinas, Bentham and Burke. They find clear evidence to support their anxieties in the statistics available since the foundation of the Athenaeum relating to social, medical, demographic, manufacturing, importing and exporting activities, production and consumption of Great Britain. Their significance accordingly finds some reflection in these pages, with their allusion to disruption and decay. When in more desperate days, the Roman Empire had been overrun and destroyed by new peoples ignorant of Homer, Plato, Aristotle, Cicero, Virgil and Horace, a Bishop of the early Christian Church among the Visigoths, not notable for his exceptional wisdom, wrote to a friend in A.D. 478 saying 'the tempest of war has wrecked the Roman power' and 'since old grades of rank are now abolished which once distinguished the high from the low, in future culture must afford the sole criterion of ability'. Western civilisation today may not be thought to need that insight, but it is relevant to every society because all have to educate successive younger generations. They are likely to do so more successfully by remembering the Bishop's words. As this survey has shown, his principle finds reflection in the manner in which the Athenaeum was established and has been maintained in being since 1824.

Notwithstanding high claims of a somewhat philosophical character in explanation of the great strength of the Club spirit, there were signs in the early twentieth century that in common with almost all London Clubs, the Athenaeum was already beginning to experience the effects of changes in social habits and customs that are generally supposed to have come to light in our own day and not before. In 1911 Ralph Nevill, that keen chronicler of the Edwardian social world of London, was writing about 'that spirit of vitality which seems within the last two decades to have deserted so many London Clubs'. No contemporary technological invention can be cited to explain why such a change was already apparent in 1911. Radio, broadcasting, television, the motor-car, the cinema and other modern leisure-hour interests did not then lure men from their Clubs. Everything that contributed to attracting men to join together in founding and maintaining Clubs still seemed to remain unchanged. Suburbs were spreading beyond the countryside in which villages such as Dulwich, Clapham Common, Blackheath and Eltham were set among fields and hedgerows, yet the population of central London was vastly greater in 1911 than it had been half a century or more previously. When the Athenaeum building was ready in 1830 about one and three-quarter million men, women and children lived in London. In 1911 when Nevill commented upon the decline in the popularity of London Clubs, there were over four and a half million in the county of London alone. Over England and Wales as a whole the increase was from just under fourteen millions in 1831 to just over thirty-six millions in 1911.

How restricted life could be for vast numbers of Londoners in the early days of the Athenaeum was illustrated by one of Theodore Hook's stories of a winter's evening journey from Bishopsgate in the City to Kilburn. In that short distance of between three and four miles, it was necessary to pass through nine tollgates.

The Coffee Room.

Ballot Day, 1892.

See page 141 *for key.*

Michael Faraday.

1. Lord Justice Denman.
2. Bishop of London.
3. Duke of Argyll.
4. Mr. Lecky.
5. Canon Farrar.
6. Sir Arthur Sullivan.
7. Dr. Quain.
8. Professor Seeley.
9. Bishop of Winchester.
10. Bishop of Gloucester.
11. Dr. Stainer.
12. Lord Hannen.
13. Dean Bradley.
14. Sir F. Burton.
15. Lord Justice Fry.
16. Sir Charles Hallé.
17. Lord Esher.
18. Justice North.
19. Justice Chitty.
20. Lord Dufferin.
21. Lord Knutsford.
22. Rt. Hon. Hugh Childers.
23. Mr. Speaker Peel.
24. Professor Huxley.
25. Archbishop of Canterbury.
26. Lord Lorne.
27. Bishop of Oxford.
28. Lord Playfair.
29. Bishop of Manchester.
30. Justice Hawkins.
31. Mr. John Evans.
32. Lord Chief Justice.
33. Bishop of Newcastle.
34. Lord Northbrook.
35. Professor Stokes.
36. Mr. H. R. Tedder (Secretary).
37. Canon Duckworth.
38. Dr. Vaughan.
39. Sir John Gilbert.
40. Sir John Lubbock.
41. Mr. John Morley.
42. Mr. Alma-Tadema.
43. Sir Theodore Martin.
44. Lord Kelvin.
45. Mr. G. J. Goschen.
46. Sir Henry Rawlinson.
47. Sir F. Leighton.
48. Baron Pollock.
49. Bishop of Chichester.
50. Sir Rutherford Alcock.
51. Mr. Shaw-Lefevre.
52. Lord Carlingford.
53. Lord Selborne.
54. Mr. Herbert Spencer.
55. Sir Joseph Lister.
56. Sir F. Abel.
57. Lord Sherbrooke.
58. Archbishop of York.
59. Mr. Andrew Lang.

KEY TO LARGE ENGRAVING—THE ATHENÆUM CLUB: BALLOT DAY.

In pouring rain or snow the traveller had to dismount and to fumble for the fee. If the return journey was made after midnight it was necessary to pay again. Bad money among the change in the dark was a minor evil compared with the danger from lurking gangs of footpads, while the risk of accidents in the dark was an ever-present hazard. After about 1850 these obstacles to travel were fairly speedily abolished, but even by 1911, when Nevill wrote, there was far less journeying about the country than there is today, when all Britain seems to be on wheels. Already then, however, some people were beginning to make a habit of leaving London on Friday or Saturday, returning on Sunday night or Monday morning, but 'le week-end' and 'la semaine anglaise' were still relative novelties enjoyed mainly by the guests at the great country-house parties. By no means all the very many more professional men, the potential or actual Members of London Clubs, were regular week-enders.

The general level of wealth and leisure was much higher in 1911 than it had been when the great Club began. Despite serious crises and setbacks, England had prospered during the nineteenth century. By the 1890's real wages were about double what they had been at the beginning of the century, while the average price level had been halved. Poverty was still grim, but the poor were not that unrelieved mass of crushed and sunken people who broke Matthew Arnold's heart as he sallied forth from the Athenaeum to work among them and for them as one of Her Majesty's Inspectors of Schools. Industrial and business enterprise driven by immense energy and private initiative in the pursuit of profit, the 'self-help' of Samuel Smiles, had, despite excesses, inhumanity and relentless self-seeking, at last begun to alleviate the worst evils of the appalling over-population (in relation to the productive capacity of the nation at that time), by which Victorian England had been cursed. Accompanying enormous economic progress and a vast increase in the wealth of the country, some fundamental change began in the way of life of those who had profited most in the race for prosperity. It was a new attitude or set of social habits that began to affect almost all Clubs adversely, although in the oldest and more famous, such as the Athenaeum, life still went on in its accustomed serene and leisurely way. There was still a long waiting-list of candidates for admission who would cheerfully have paid a higher entrance fee and a greater annual subscription if by so doing they could have gained admission. In 1872 the Travellers' Club was similarly beset with a thousand candidates on the waiting-list which meant a delay of about twelve years before election. Yet a falling-off in the number of meals served there was already causing concern then, and again in 1889. A similar decline in the number of diners had been reported in 1885.

Preoccupied as many Clubs must be today with grave difficulties arising mainly from ruinous inflation, it will be surprising to learn that in 1914 already, before the outbreak of the First World War, J. H. S. Escott, writing of *Club Makers and Club Members* thought that the great days of London Clubs were over. 'Whether social, or political, imperial or domestic, club creation has now done its work and reached its goal', he said. He foresaw a 'further reversion to type in the shape of a return to the tavern clubs'.

Endeavouring to account for this change in social habits, he attributed it to the habit of week-ending and the competition of

> rivals daily growing in popularity like the legion of first-class restaurants, none of which was in existence fifty years ago, while some of the best known like the 'Ritz' and the 'Savoy', however famous and firmly established, are even more modern growths. [Because of 'the innovation' of weekends] much that gave the nineteenth century Carlton and Reform real interest and importance has disappeared . . . the great Saturday and Sunday dinners at the joint-stock palaces of Pall Mall or St. James's have therefore gone. At the height of the Session [of Parliament] and the Season, the Athenaeum, the Travellers' and St. Stephen's Club, so convenient for gentlemen of the long robe with parliamentary practice, are scarcely less deserted than during September or on Christmas Day.

While it is probably true that both restaurants and week-ending had serious effects on Clubs, they cannot explain all the difficulties of many Clubs, even if they adequately accounted for the troubles before 1914, which seems unlikely. Absence on Saturday and Sunday does not explain the relative emptiness of Club dining-rooms on weekdays. (After the Catering and Wages Act the Athenaeum closed on Sundays. For over ten years it and 'The Senior' used to close on alternate Sundays, acting as each other's host when open, but when 'The Senior' decided in 1960 not to open on Sundays, the Athenaeum then also closed.) Among the additional millions populating London it might have been expected that the proportion of men likely to value the amenities of Club life would not be significantly smaller than it had been when several favoured Clubs had over a thousand names on their waiting-lists. Family life had then begun to change; husbands and fathers seem to have returned home after a day's work with an alacrity that those who filled Club dining-rooms before 1900 did not exhibit. Vast numbers now have much further to travel as the congested car-parks of railway stations within a forty- or fifty-mile radius from London and the appalling rush-hour congestion of the railways and highways to London daily demonstrate. If there was then a considerable proportion of bachelors or widowers among those crowds, they are not likely to be less numerous today. Many such may now take their main meal of the day at lunch, being content with a light meal at night, but then the total number of meals served in Clubs should not have continually diminished over thirty years. Club Members who are active in professions or business are unlikely to be attracted by office canteens, or staff lunch rooms, neither are they in the luncheon-voucher category who have to limit their choice of restaurants. In the evenings it is understandable that the younger generation may find that the animation and *réclame* of a fashionable restaurant has more glamour than a Ladies' Annexe at dinner-time, while the necessity in a Club to eat before 8.30 p.m. may often be another restrictive condition. When, however, the cost of a restaurant meal is compared with that in a Club, it is likely always to be greater. Despite the dubious repute attaching to the *cuisine* of the Athenaeum it is doubtful if that of the average restaurant is much better at the same price. Restaurants, moreover, do not provide the amenities of a drawing-room, a library or a lounge in which diners can linger with a book, a periodical, or to talk. A decline in the number of meals served is but one symptom of that general falling off in the popularity of Clubs that has caused many to close their doors and has prevented the creation of new Clubs. Whether the number of restricted dining-clubs meeting in taverns, hotels and restaurants has considerably increased, as Mr. Escott assumed it would, probably cannot be discovered. Some of them are now able to reserve a room at a West End Club if one or more of their number is a Member, and several do so meet, particularly now that ladies are admitted to several Clubs in the evening.

There is, therefore, clear evidence that nineteenth-century enthusiasm for all that Clubs had to offer had waned considerably by the beginning of the twentieth century, although the Athenaeum had not suffered. Then came the frightful catastrophe of the First World War. From this also the Athenaeum may seem to have emerged relatively less diminished than other Clubs, notably 'The Senior' with its membership of serving or reserve officers, and other Clubs whose Members were younger than those of the Athenaeum. Nevertheless the Athenaeum could not but be afflicted by the ghastly loss to the nation of the flower of its youth – 'the lost generation'. In the mud of Flanders, in graves in Salonika, and the Middle East, in the seven seas, lay the bones of the men who would have become famous authors, artists, lawyers, judges, bishops, Fellows of the Royal and other Societies, future holders of the Order of Merit, some of whom would undoubtedly have strengthened the Athenaeum. Again a heavy blow fell in 1939–45. From these two major disasters recovery could not but be slow. Pessimists fear that just as the ultimate decline of victorious Rome can be traced to its disastrous struggle for life against the might of Carthage, so despite its hard-won victory, England seemed, not without glory, to have been knocked out of the world race for prosperity and achievement. By September 1972, a generation had succeeded those who had won undying fame in the Battle of Britain, but in the task bequeathed to them by the slain, to win back prosperity for their war-shattered country too many faltered and failed. When the economic achievement of twenty countries was then compared, the United Kingdom ranked at the very bottom of the table with Puerto Rico, Libya and Southern Italy. National productivity per head of the population in the United Kingdom was less than half that of the United States and Sweden; one the home of free enterprise, the other a socialist, planned, Welfare State. The countries defeated and shattered by the war in which Great Britain was victorious, had already outstripped the victor in industry, trade and commerce.

Changes in social habits and in the way of life; years of desperate warfare to defend that way of life; colossal losses in men and fortune; successive national near-bankruptcies, devaluations and inflation; greed, envy and selfishness fomented by demagogues as a basis for public policy dividing the nation and blunting the will to create; militant aggressiveness in the pursuit of private advantages; an insistence upon alleged rights but silence upon personal duties; 'demonstrations'; violence, increasing crime and sexual indulgence – such salient features of life in Great Britain contrast too strongly with the Victorian era for even a naïve optimist to remain complacent. As though blind to the paramount need to create wealth to repair the ravages of war, British politics was geared to the enjoyment of wealth, to the urge to spend and consume. In 1972, 64 per cent, nearly two-thirds of the total national expenditure of the United Kingdom, was devoted to personal consumption: the highest percentage in Europe and it was rising by 2 per cent per annum. In Germany, the next highest, the percentage was 54 only, and it had been virtually static at that amount.

Members of the Athenaeum of a century and more ago would deplore it all as a disastrous example of the havoc that demagogic politics can inflict upon a once powerful nation. Temporarily sustaining illusions of prosperity, the national currency was depreciated, with crippling consequences for cultural life, some of which have already been indicated. No pessimistic assessment of Great Britain's productive energies should be allowed to withhold ample and grateful recognition of the strenuous efforts made by the more energetic élite among workers and managers who create and build up new industries and who improve traditional production, making it possible to carry the immense burden of sustaining a reasonable standard of living both for those who do not work to their full capacity and for some who do not work at all. Many toil long into the night, so the executives, managers and professional men among them cannot take their ease in their Club after the 5 p.m.–6 p.m. contingent has gone home.

But already, before inflation had wreaked all the havoc it has since spread far and wide throughout the nation, a writer in *The Times* (4 May 1956) foresaw 'growing difficulties ahead for club Committees'. It is doubtful whether at that time the alarming rate of depreciation of the currency and its sinister effects were foreseen. Merely as matters then stood, the problem of maintaining a Club on an even keel appeared to be difficult enough, so it is not surprising that subsequent economic hurricanes rocked many a club violently and overturned others. In 1956 already, the writer in *The Times* observed that 'if club Committees put subscriptions up, members resign. If they reduce wages, the staff resign.' Today it would be said 'unless they continually raise wages, the staff resign'. No way out of this dilemma was seen. There were, it was said, 'too many clubs for the potential club population'. If this were true, it points to an as yet unexplained change in the character, or the cultural interests, or the habits, of the immensely greater population of the country. For there are still as many, if not more, judges, bishops, Fellows of the Royal Society, of the Royal Academy, the British Academy and other learned societies as there used to be when they queued for election to the Athenaeum before 1914, while as for professors, active or retired, there were never so many as there are today. Never has the pursuit of learning and science, the cultivation of the arts and music, had more aspirants. In some arts a veritable renaissance has been hailed as British sculpture, music, printing, and the art of the theatre have won international renown. Inflation has diminished the real income of many men active in cultural matters, but not all have suffered alike, for the earnings of the more fortunate do not invariably lag as inflation rushes ahead. That Club Members are as unsympathetic as ever to any increase in annual subscriptions should be less likely in these days when every money cost rises. Yet none can have any difficulty in understanding the effect of inflation upon the cost of maintaining the Club. The simple principle on which all Club Committees must resolutely act at all times, is to raise subscriptions without question whenever it is necessary to meet rising costs and to lower subscriptions if they produce an income far in excess of the Club's needs. No shifts or expedients designed to avert the necessity of raising subscriptions to match inflationary increases in costs are worth a moment's consideration. Merging with another Club or widening the membership by the admission of women as full Members are alternatives tried elsewhere, not always with success. Unless a Club once accustomed to maintaining a good if not high standard in the matter of food and service is resolute to sustain its good name, it is questionable whether it deserves to survive. Minor cheese-paring economies irritate Members and induce a defeatist spirit. Their cumulative effect is inevitably to suggest that the Club is running down. When once that feeling arises, worse evils are more difficult to avert. Members may look with envy at other Clubs where better standards are maintained. If they do not, potential candidates will. Entries in the Candidates Book then decline, and all because Club Committees, terrified by the ravages of inflation, shrink from raising subscriptions in order to maintain standards. Their defeatist attitude is itself a bad sign. They have no faith in their Members' loyalty, or, in economic terms, they judge their elasticity of demand for what the Club has to offer to be unlikely to sustain the cost of maintaining it. In all situations of danger Nelson's principle alone is sound, 'engage the enemy more closely'. It is a principle that must apply with particular force in the Athenaeum and other Clubs which stand or fall by excellence in their service and by their determination to uphold the highest standards of achievement in the arts and sciences and in the life of the mind. It will be a bad day for their Members and also for Great Britain if they fail in that great task, that clear duty. If that day should ever come, then all those loyal to the values and traditions that inspired the Club's foundation and early prosperity would regretfully have to decide to bring it to an end so as to spare themselves and the world an ignominious spectacle of a once honoured edifice from which the spirit had departed.

Any attempt to arrive at an opinion about the probable future of London Clubs inevitably involves all the problems, economic, political, social and cultural that arise in relation to the future of Great Britain generally. Here it is not possible to do more than merely to refer to those most closely pertinent to the Athenaeum. It is, as observed at the beginning of this historical sketch, avowedly a Club for an élite, in the ordinary dictionary meaning of that word, as there explained. As such, it inevitably incurs the spleen of demagogues, as all West End Clubs of London are liable to do also. For as Mr. Percy Colson observed in his history of White's, 'It is the genius of the few – poets, writers, artists, the designers of beautiful streets and buildings, that makes a nation civilized. These never have been, are not, and never will be democratic.' Whether such classes had 'understanding support' in eighteenth-century England, as he supposed, is a more dubious view of social history. It was not so much the 'support' of the poorer classes as their and everybody's age-old belief that inequality is part of the ineluctable nature of things, that delayed the demagogues' assault on the rich. Mr. Colson was on firmer ground in pointing out that 'it is not for their social services and their subservience to *hoi polloi* that Greece and Rome live in history'. In those far-off days the idea that society as a whole had any evident daily responsibility for the welfare of individuals was rejected with reasoned patience by Aristotle and more summarily by others, such as Cicero. To conclude from such a historical example that Greece and Rome would not have lived in history had they invented the Welfare State, would be another argument. If by the word 'democratic' Mr Colson intended to imply that a Club should open its doors to all and sundry, he is correct in supposing that such a step would destroy the Club. The belief that this disaster will never happen, must rest upon the same faith that sees Great Britain ready to take a great leap forward in all spheres of activity.

In creating a Welfare State, the British gave practical form to the faith that with better health, nourishment, housing, education, and all other social services, many more opportunities would be provided for talent to emerge than when genius had to make its way unaided. So today British children begin their school life younger and leave it older by two years than they were mostly forced to do a generation ago. New technical colleges, universities and other institutes of learning are spread throughout the British Isles. Broadcasting and television give millions of people of all ages tremendous opportunities to enlarge their mental horizons. Books as 'paperbacks' have enormously expanded the market for serious writing as well as for pulp fiction.

Many see the result of so vast an expansion as involving initially a lowering of standards, because 'more inevitably means worse' when the culturally under-developed have to be catered for by 'mass media' that were once produced for a smaller, more cultivated circle. They now must widen their appeal or perish, it seems, so Britain lacks a daily newspaper as 'adult' as *Le Monde* that so far has not been compelled to court a public attracted by the latest events in the life of a footballer or film actress with pictures to match, often as sexually stimulating as possible without appearing objectionably lascivious.

Optimists tolerate such lowered cultural standards in the hope that a far broader basis is being provided than ever before, upon which a very much more worthy cultural life for vastly more people will in time grow and flourish.

As this historical survey of the Athenaeum, one institution created by and for a cultural élite, has shown, it will be nothing new if many of its Members emerge from the social levels characterised by Mr. Colson as *hoi polloi*. Faraday, Chantrey, Gould and others were early examples, while as for the present day, one or two at least among the Members would not be able to produce much more in the way of gilt-edged credentials without having attained anything like their eminence.

Unless men and women of superior ability emerge to devote their talents to invention, organisation and leadership, the outlook for the millions constantly being added to the population of a small country such as Great Britain, all of them dependent upon their ability to earn their livelihood by creating exports, visible and otherwise, could be exceedingly sombre. Again 'The Song of the Shirt' could be heard to cause tears to flow once more for misery without a cure. Moreover within the foreseeable future, some suppose that half the population will be the descendants of today's and yesterday's immigrants whose social and cultural traditions are not British; the same situation as that of Imperial Rome.

If popular expectations of constantly rising standards are disappointed; if present standards decline as inflation is at last seen to provoke, instead of to stave off disaster; if higher taxes on incomes and expenditure further discourage saving and depress enterprise, demagogues will shout louder for 'the taxation of wealth' because they are impotent to promote its creation. What is left of the savings and investments of former generations may then also be pillaged to be spent as 'income'. Many treasures, once private possessions, have been forced upon the market already; mostly exported to pay huge levies on capital in the shape of 'death duties'. Used as income by the State, they can be regarded as having bought beer and tobacco for the millions of recipients of State aid, because these two commodities continue to figure among the heaviest single items of consumers' expenditure. How long then would it be before the cry 'down with privilege', 'away with élites' added the buildings and the pictures, books and silver of the great Clubs to those already auctioned off to postpone the day of reckoning? Whether such possibilities are ever likely to become probabilities, and whether the ensuing collapse can be averted, are sinister problems for the coming generation to resolve.

Pessimists therefore do not lack reasons for fearing that there may be no celebration of the first two hundred years of the Athenaeum in A.D. 2024. Optimists can reply with but one answer; one resolve, the one quoted already, that cannot be too often repeated. 'Engage the enemy more closely.' Nelson's motto must fortify the faith that the attack on poverty, ignorance, envy, greed, hatred and violence and all other evils against which the energies of sane publicists and politicians in the environment of the Welfare State are directed, will, if well managed, within measurable time, and for the first time, so raise all standards that the virtues and qualities which the Athenaeum and other Clubs have fostered for a century and a half will be increasingly understood and prized, because the need for them will be seen to be ever greater. Then their enduring prosperity and steady progress will be ensured as they too benefit from that social welfare and cultural advancement which their Members have already so long and so successfully striven to promote.

One Hundred and Fiftieth Anniversary Dinner
23 May, 1974

To mark the 150th Anniversary of the founding of the Club a Dinner, attended by 176 Members, was held in the Club House. His Royal Highness the Duke of Edinburgh (Honorary Life Member) was in the Chair and proposed 'The Club'. The Lord Morris of Borth-y-Gest replied.

His Royal Highness The Duke of Edinburgh's Speech

I have no doubt that all members are well aware of the fact that this Club was instituted 'for the association of individuals known for their scientific or literary attainments, artists of eminence in any class of the fine arts, and noblemen and gentlemen distinguished as liberal patrons of science, literature or the arts'. I only repeat this quotation because it ought to give all members present on this 150th anniversary dinner a pleasant glow of pride and satisfaction. Whatever the world may think about them at other times, at least the Athenaeum recognises their true merit. If that is not enough to soothe the ego, I can think of nothing better to restore morale than to read through the list of distinguished people who have graced the Club with their membership.

On the occasion of the centenary dinner in 1924, the then Archbishop of Canterbury, Archbishop Davidson, seems to have felt a similar sensation. He put it this way 'Think of the good it does to experience the Club's 'hob-nobbing' and how excellent it is to get in touch with greater lights whose conversation can flash colour and poetry into our drab prosaic levels; how it helps to break down the grooviness and narrowness; and on the other hand, it cannot fail to do good for the great folk in science, literature and art to come down occasionally to earth by mixing with the lesser lights'.

I must say, I rather like the idea of an Archbishop of Canterbury counting himself among the lesser lights and living at a drab prosaic level. But then the Archbishop, in the same speech, said that he had been told by one of his examiners that 'it is a good thing you have application, Sir, for you certainly have no ability'.

Social clubs have always tended to bring together people with a common interest or a common occupation. The Senior – by nine years – across the road, for example, was founded for naval and military gentlemen. Then there is the Jockey Club and the yacht clubs, some of which were founded in the eighteenth century.

In modern times there are political clubs, motoring clubs, tennis clubs, in fact I am sure there is a club for every human activity. Among all this lot the Athenaeum is almost unique in that the founders saw the advantage of bringing people together, who were distinguished in a number of only loosely related interests and occupations. Unless, of course, it were to be claimed that the uncommon denominator for membership was intellectual brilliance.

I suspect that the importance of this mixing of intellects and occupations at the centre of a nation's life is inclined to be overlooked. We have seen so many instances of artificial capital cities specially constructed to house the central government in convenience and dignity. It may be a planner's dream, but in human terms and in terms of national leadership it is less satisfactory.

There is strong evidence that the quality of government suffers where legislators and administrators are socially cut-off from their equals in business, the professions or the arts assuming, of course, that they have any equals in these enlightened, egalitarian days.

It is fifty years since the Club celebrated 100 years of happy existence. I think most commentators today would be inclined to say that the last fifty years have witnessed some of the greatest changes this country or the world have ever experienced. On the other hand, perhaps the French are a bit more perceptive, for they have a saying that the more things change, the more they remain the same. I was rather struck by this idea while I was reading what Sir Reginald Blomfield said at that dinner fifty years ago.

'For instance,' he said '. . . the prestige of the stage has been steadily rising so that now it shares with the Bar the proud distinction of occupying more space in the daily papers than anything else except the racing news and quotations on the Stock Exchange.' For 'stage' read 'pop-idols' and his comment would be quite up to date.

A bit further on he referred to revolutionaries in art:—'They fluttered the dove-cotes to such purpose that the doves are still flapping about uncertain where to alight. So after impressionism, we had cubism, futurism, vorticism, significant form and the reduction ad absurdism of the whole thing; non-representational art'. The only difference today is that there do not appear to be any doves to do any flapping, or if there are they have become like the three wise monkeys – 'see no art, hear no music, make no comment about the Arts Council'.

Mr. Chairman, as an Honorary Life Member of twenty-one years standing, this occasion obviously has a rather special personal significance, but I would like to say that nothing could have given me greater pleasure than to be asked to propose the toast to the Club on this historic occasion. I do not think I could do better than to propose this toast in words used by that same Archbishop fifty years ago, because I believe it expresses the feelings of all the members today as accurately as it did when he used them:—

'The supreme thankfulness for what I at least have found gain – recreation, uplift which is afforded by the Club of which we are so proud – a Club which is both seed, plot and cementing of friendships precious to us all.'

I would like to ask everyone present to join me in a toast to the continuing vitality and success of the Athenaeum Club.

Lord Morris of Borth-y-Gest's speech

Your Royal Highness, Your Grace, My Lords and gentlemen. When on one occasion Her Majesty Queen Victoria accepted an invitation from the then Duke of Sutherland to his stately London home, which now for many years we have known as Lancaster House, it is said that being greeted on arrival Her Majesty remarked, 'I come from my house to your palace.' Sir, we are very delighted that tonight you should have come from your palace to your Club to give us your fellow members the privilege of dining under your chairmanship and the pleasure of hearing your speech. I am very deeply sensible of the honour which is mine at this moment of being our spokesman to express our gratitude to you, Sir. I am quite sure that I speak for all my fellow members when I say, as I do very respectfully, that you, Sir, have indeed worthily, discerningly and very happily paid tribute to our Club in this very special year.

We know, I think, quite a lot about those who were our founders. We know rather more about them I think than we do about our sublime Goddess Athena herself. Of her we have read. We have read that when her father Zeus learnt that his wife Metis was going to have a second child, he consumed her: his strange and rather unorthodox behaviour being attributable to the fact that he had learned that a second child would be more powerful than he was and might dethrone him. When later Prometheus split open Zeus's brow, out stepped Athena fully armed. Sir, the Family Planning Association had better not get to know of this!

But I think that tonight we can express our satisfaction with all that was done by John Wilson Croker, the virtual founder of this Club – Member of Parliament, Privy Councillor, Secretary of the Admiralty. We are very glad that he wrote a letter to Sir Humphry Davy, the President of the Royal Society, and that they got together a distinguished group which included Chantrey the sculptor, Thomas Moore the poet and very many other distinguished people, amongst whom was Sir Walter Scott. And so they founded the Club. At first we were called, I think, 'The Society'. I don't know, Sir, whether there will be any move to change our name again. What would be suggested? The Establishment? Sir, I hope that we will keep the name 'The Athenaeum'. But I am sure that those present who can speak with expert knowledge will feel that that distinguished group did a fine piece of work when they recruited Decimus Burton to build this lovely Club house. Decimus Burton was only twenty-four when the Club was formed. He was twenty-six when he was commissioned to build this house.

Croker was a very forcible personality. We know of the clashes he had with Macaulay in the House of Commons. Macaulay, I read the other day, writing to his sister said, 'I detest Croker. I detest him more than I do cold roast veal.' Many of us I think could suggest candidates for detestation with greater claims than cold roast veal! So we got under way.

The Duke of Wellington, of course, was one of our early members. He was a member of The Senior, to which you have referred, Sir, and doubtless of The Union Club and of other clubs. When we go out of our door and see the horse block outside and when we read the inscription on it, 'This horse block was erected by desire of The Duke of Wellington 1830', we might be tempted to think that the Duke had a preference for the Athenaeum over The Senior! But then we have to remind ourselves that exactly opposite and outside The Senior is a horse block containing the inscription, 'This horse block was erected by desire of The Duke of Wellington 1830'.

We have always been on good terms with The Senior. Taxi drivers had their names for the two of us. At one stage they called us 'Bishopsgate' and they called The Senior 'Cripplegate'. Another bracket of names was to call us 'The Mental' and The Senior 'The Regimental'. I think that when they called us 'The Mental' they meant it kindly and not in its present rather flippant derogatory sense.

We may ask why does a man join a club? Dr Johnson had his thoughts: but he thought mainly of a tavern. 'No, sir, there is nothing which has yet been contrived by man by which so much happiness has been produced as by a good tavern.' He would be a bold man who referred to the Athenaeum as a tavern! But here we have no political party to favour, no special cause to espouse. Here is a place where kindred spirits gather together. We are happy and proud to meet those with whom we may here be in association. Matthew Arnold referred to the Club as 'a place where I enjoy something resembling beatitude'.

I heard of a man from the provinces who on his occasional visits to London had great happiness if he could spot celebrities: then he would go home and say 'I saw so and so, or so and so.' One day when walking down Whitehall he saw somebody of distinguished appearance approaching him: he went up to him and said, 'Pardon me, sir, but are you anybody in particular?' Every member of the Athenaeum is somebody in particular. Indeed if one was dining in this room and if one did not know who one's neighbour was and happened to ask him to pass the salt, for all one might know he could be a scientist of worldwide reputation who knew more about the chemical properties of salt than any other living person.

Here we share the same approach to the art of living: perhaps I can say that we are all fairly reserved, rather modest and quite self-controlled. No one in this Club would ever be of the imperious or assertive type. I heard of one such who was dining, not here, but in a very different place: he was very conscious of his own importance and he thought that the waiter was not quite paying him the attention and the deference that were his due. He said to the waiter, 'Do you know who I am?' The waiter with perfect civility said, 'No, sir, but if you will wait a moment, sir, I will make some inquiries and let you know.'

Tonight perhaps we can permit ourselves a little vanity and a little pride. When the Order of Merit was established in, I think, the year 1902, no fewer than eleven of the recipients of that very high Order were members of this Club. We did what is a very good thing for a Club to do. We had a dinner. The dinner was in this room and we entertained Lord Roberts, Lord Kitchener, Admiral Keppel, Admiral Seymour, Sir William Huggins, G. F. Watts, John Morley, Lord Wolseley, Lord Rayleigh, Lord Kelvin and Lord Lister. Are we not allowed to be a little proud of them? Lord Avebury presided and Mr. A. J. Balfour made a speech at the end of dinner (which I may say consisted of ten courses). During the speeches the company, sipping their port, were drinking Dow's '75. It was then that Mr A. J. Balfour, referring to the company gathered in this room, said that 'probably never before in a room of this size had there been gathered together a company of such undiluted eminence.'

Of our library we need not conceal our pride. It would be perhaps misunderstood if I said that in our library there is a wonderful store of knowledge and all of it well shelved! It was in the library that Thackeray did so much of his work. Macaulay, in the corner near the books on history, did much of his writing. At the centre table Richard Burton sat translating 'The Arabian Nights'. Those who used the library included Hallam, Sir Henry Maine, Matthew Arnold, Mark Pattison, Lord Acton and dozens of others. Trollope, I think, did most of his writing in the drawing-room, and I think it was in the south corner of the drawing-room. Those who were at the Annual General Meeting a few days ago must wonder what his reaction might have been to proposals concerning Lady Guests in the Club but it wouldn't have been as drastic as was the course that he proposed when, overhearing a conversation between two clergymen who considered that he was using some characters, and one in particular, rather too much, he said, 'Well, I will go home and I promise you that within a few days I will kill Mrs Proudie.'

Dickens, I think, did much of his writing in the library. We have there a chair presented by one of our members which was bought at Gadd's Hill Place. Dickens had been sitting on it when writing *Edwin Drood*. Such was the precision and the quality of perfection of our members that when the chair was given, a little brass plate was put on it recording the fact that it was bought by auction at Gadd's Hill Place: but not only that, the date of the auction was recorded: it was the 10th August, 1870: and furthermore the lot number in the sale was recorded: it was lot number 277. On the chair is an exhortation from the Committee which invites us not to sit on it. We are law-abiding: I have never seen anyone sitting on the chair. It would be churlish for me to add that for some years past the seat has been in a collapsed condition.

Here then has been no mere coterie of friends idling in a backwater. Here there have been leaders and those who have set the tone and the pattern of our public life. Here have been those who have been original thinkers who have influenced thought the world over. We might almost say in the words of the Psalmist, 'There is neither speech nor language but their voices are heard among them, their sound is gone out into all the lands and their words unto the ends of the world.'

Naturally when we study the history of a club we learn of certain characters. May I say that I am very delighted to know that a new history of the Club, coming from the erudite pen of Dr Cowell, will shortly be available for us. I don't know whether we have characters today. They say there are no characters. But I don't know, Sir. Perhaps we are all characters. In any event, better to be a character than to be colourless. One such of whom I have read was that remarkable man, Abraham Hayward who was connected with *The Times* and with two leading quarterlies. He had his own seat in this room and probably in the drawing-room also. Woe betide anyone who took his place! I think one place was known as 'Hayward's Heath', and the other as 'Abraham's Bosom'! He was one of those daring men who played a game called whist. He was a very good player but on one occasion he revoked. We are told that when the news of it came, the news was received throughout the Club with 'a hum of awestruck satisfaction'! It was he who at the time of Convocation, or Church Assembly, whichever would be the right description, said 'Ah, I see the bishops are beginning to swarm. The atmosphere is charged with them. Every moment I expect to find one dropping into my soup.'

May I say that we are always very delighted when we see our Archbishops and our Bishops in the Club. I hope it will not be thought presumptuous if I say how delighted we are that Her Majesty The Queen should have nominated our fellow member, Dr Coggan, for election to succeed another fellow member as Archbishop of Canterbury.

We have respect for our Bishops. In such circumstances as the following they deserve our sympathy. A bishop delivered a splendid address in a certain locality. He illustrated his theme by some admirable and apt stories. The Press at the end wished to check with him on one or two references. It occurred to the bishop that he had to give another address shortly and that one or two of the stories that he had told might again be apt. 'It would be very helpful if those stories were not reproduced in the paper. Might the Press be willing to co-operate?' Yes, the Press were willing to co-operate. The bishop was very pleased with an admirable newspaper report of his speech, subject only to one sentence in it. That read 'during his address the bishop told three or four stories. Unhappily they are stories that we cannot print.'

Sir, we regard name-dropping as a mild social foible which we can excuse with the tolerance of a benevolent disdain. I hope that I will not be accused of name-dropping if tonight I mention a few of the giants of the past. If there were giants in those days, well, it is no bad thing to look up to giants: and so if we thought of Robert Browning or Thomas Carlyle or John Stuart Mill or Ruskin or Herbert Spencer or Kipling or T. S. Eliot or Gilbert Murray or Russell or Trevelyan, it would not be that we had forgotten Irving or Kemble or Kean or Squire Bancroft or that, though we omit on these occasions famous prime ministers and mighty leaders in war, we had failed to remember such great men as John Bright and Richard Cobden and the Earl of Shaftesbury. Flitting to another field we might mention Giles Gilbert Scott, Sir John Millais, J. W. M. Turner, Burne-Jones, Lawrence, Leighton, Lutyens, Gerald Kelly or, flitting again, Bishop Wilberforce, Archbishop Tait, Archbishop Lord Lang, Archbishop William Temple, or, flitting again, Barry, Stamp, Sterndale, Bennett,

Sullivan, Elgar or, shall I say, Charles Darwin or Huxley, or Charles Sherrington or Fleming. These are but examples of names that could be multiplied.

Sir, I have said that each one of us who is a member here is proud to be a member. But with that pride there must be some measure of humility. That comes when we remember that in this place have found contentment so many who, with high distinction, have served their monarch, their country and their generation: so many who have enlarged the frontiers of knowledge: so many who have added to the riches of our literature: so many who have had a zest for style and grace and beauty: so many who in various ways have been on the side of the forces of good in their eternal struggle with the powers of evil. Of the work of all those we have become the inheritors. May those who come after us also be inheritors.

Sir, again we thank you. You have made this evening an occasion to remember.

Appendices

Note on Trustees

In the original Rules of the Club (1824) the Trustees consisted of the President of the Royal Society, the President of the Society of Antiquaries, the President of the Royal Academy and two other Members of the Club elected by the Committee.

In 1876 the Rules were altered and the Trustees consisted of three Members elected by the Committee. The Presidents of the Royal Society, the Society of Antiquaries and the Royal Society were no longer *ex-officio* Trustees, but became *ex-officio* Members of the General Committee.

In 1936 the Rules were again altered and the number of Trustees was changed from three to not more than five.

Below is given a list of the Trustees giving names of the Trustees and the dates of their Trusteeship as far as can be ascertained from the records:

Name	*Dates*
Sir Humphry Davy (PRS)	1824–1828
Sir Thomas Lawrence (PRA)	1824–1830
Lord Aberdeen (PSA)	1824–1846
John Wilson Croker	1824–1857
Edmund Hopkinson	1824–1825
Richard Heber	1825–1828
Davies Gilbert (PRS)	1828–1839
Lord Farnborough	1828–1838
Sir Martin Archer Shee (PRA)	1830–1850
Lord Shaftesbury	1838–1852
Marquess of Northampton (PRS)	1841–1851
Viscount Mahon, aft. Earl Stanhope (PSA)	1846–1875
Sir Charles Eastlake (PRA)	1850–1865
Earl of Rosse (PRS)	1852–1854
Lord Wharncliffe	1852–1855
Lord Wrottesley (PRS)	1854–1857

Name	*Dates*
Lord Overstone	1857–1883
Sir Roderick Murchison	1858–1871
Sir Benjamin Brodie (PRS)	1859–1862
Major-General Sabine (PRS)	1862–1873
Sir Francis Grant (PRA)	1865–1876
Sir J. Lubbock, aft. Lord Avebury	1874–1913
Frederic Ouvry (PSA)	1875–1881
Lord Aberdare	1881–1895
Sir Frederick A. Abel	1883–1902
Sir M. E. Grant Duff	1895–1906
Sir R. H. Collins, aft. Lord Collins	1903–1911
Field-Marshal Earl Roberts	1906–1914
Sir H. H. Cozens-Hardy, aft. Lord Cozens-Hardy	1911–1920
Randall Davidson, Archbishop of Canterbury, aft. Lord Davidson	1913–1930
Rt. Hon. A. J. Balfour	1914–1930
Lord Warrington of Clyffe	1920–1937
Rt. Hon. Stanley Baldwin, aft. Lord Baldwin	1930–1947
William Temple, Archbishop of York, aft. Canterbury	1931–1944
Lord Macmillan	1937–1952
Geoffrey Fisher, Archbishop of Canterbury	1944–1972
Sir Alan Barlow	1946–1968
Lord Simonds	1947–1971
Sir Findlater Stewart	1950–1960
Sir Cecil Carr	1952–1966
M. T. Tudsbery	1957–
Sir Alan Burns	1968–
Lord Hurcomb	1969–
Rt. Hon. Lord Parker of Waddington	1972–died 1972
Rt. Hon. F. D. Coggan, Archbishop of Canterbury	1972–
Rt. Hon. Lord Morris of Borth-y-Gest	1972–

Chairmen of the General Committee

As far as can be ascertained from the old Minutes, Annual Reports and other records there was originally no Chairman elected for a definite period. At every meeting it seems an *ad-hoc* Chairman was elected to the Chair and, in the same way, it seems the Chairman who was elected for the occasion signed the Annual Report as Chairman.

It will be seen from the list which is given below that certain Members signed the Annual Report on several occasions, but there is nothing to indicate that they were elected as Chairman for anything longer than the particular meeting. According to the Minutes of the General Committee, it would appear that the Chairman for the next twelve months was first elected in 1920 when Lord Sanderson was elected. In 1921 Lord Justice Warrington was elected, and was then re-elected in most of the following years until his retirement in 1934, and various other Chairmen have been formally elected as Chairman of the year since that date and several have been re-elected for succeeding years.

In 1935 there is the first mention of Deputy Chairman, and it was unanimously decided that a Deputy Chairman should be elected to the General Committee in addition to the Chairman each year.

It is, therefore, difficult to decide who could be officially known as the Chairman of the General Committee up to 1920. A list, however, is given below of those Members who signed the Annual Report as Chairman year by year up to 1920 and from 1920 onwards of the Members who were elected Chairman and the period for which they remained as Chairman.

Name	*Date of Signing Annual Report as Chairman*
Sir Humphry Davy, Bt.	1825
Sir Humphry Davy, Bt.	1826
Earl Spencer	1827
Davies Gilbert	1828
Rt. Hon. J. W. Croker	1829
Rt. Hon. J. W. Croker	1830
Sir Martin Archer Shee	1831
Francis Gore	1832
Thomas Peregrine Courtenay	1833
Earl Cawdor	1834
Earl Cawdor	1835

Name	*Date of Signing Annual Report as Chairman*
Rev. Christopher Benson	1836
William Richard Hamilton	1837
Earl of Shaftesbury	1838
Earl of Shaftesbury	1839
Francis Gore	1840
Lord Prudhoe	1841
Earl of Shaftesbury	1842
Lord Prudhoe	1843
Rt. Hon. William Sturges Bourne	1844
Earl of Shaftesbury	1845
Earl of Shaftesbury	1846
Earl of Shaftesbury	1847
Captain Sir George Back	1848
George Long	1849
Viscount Mahon	1850
Rt. Hon. Edward Strutt	1851
Horace Hayman Wilson	1852
Viscount Mahon	1853
Viscount Mahon	1854
Earl Stanhope	1855
Sir Roderick Murchison, Bt.	1856
Sir P. de M. Grey Egerton, Bt.	1857
Sir Roderick Murchison, Bt.	1858
Earl Stanhope	1859
Lord Overstone	1860
John Crawford	1861
Lord Overstone	1862
Earl Stanhope	1863
Sir Roderick Murchison, Bt.	1864
Earl Stanhope	1865
Earl Stanhope	1866
James Fergusson	1867
Earl Stanhope	1868
Earl Stanhope	1869
Sir Roderick Murchison, Bt.	1870
Earl Stanhope	1871
Sir John Evans	1872
John Lettsom Elliot	1873
Earl Stanhope	1874
Duke of Cleveland	1875

Name	*Date of Signing Annual Report as Chairman*
Lord Arthur Russell	1876
Frederic Ouvry	1877
Frederic Ouvry	1878
Sir Henry Yule	1879
Lord Aberdare	1880
Sir William F. Pollock, Bt.	1881
Sir William F. Pollock, Bt.	1882
Lord Aberdare	1883
Sir Frederick Abel, Bt.	1884
Sir Frederick Abel, Bt.	1885
Viscount Enfield, aft. Earl of Strafford	1886
Sir John Evans	1887
Sir John Evans	1888
Sir John Bridge	1889
Lord Aberdare	1890
Sir Frederick Abel, Bt.	1891
Lord Aberdare	1892
Sir Frederick Abel, Bt.	1893
Lord Aberdare	1894
Sir Frederick Abel, Bt.	1895
Sir Frederick Abel, Bt.	1896
Sir Frederick Abel, Bt.	1897
Viscount Knutsford	1898
Dr. M. Creighton, Bishop of London	1899
Lord Lister	1900
Lord Davey	1901
Lord Avebury	1902
Lord Avebury	1903
Lord Justice Collins	1904
Lord Justice Collins	1905
Lord Justice Collins	1906
Lord Justice Collins	1907
Lord Justice Collins	1908
Lord Justice Collins	1909
S. C. Bayley	1910
Lord Avebury	1911
Field-Marshal Earl Roberts	1912
Lord Avebury	1913
Lord Sanderson	1914
Lord Cozens-Hardy	1915

Name	*Date of Signing Annual Report as Chairman*
Lord Cozens-Hardy	1916
Lord Cozens-Hardy	1917
Viscount Mersey	1918
Viscount Mersey	1919
Lord Sanderson	1920

Name	*Elected Chairman for the Year*
Lord Sanderson	1920–1921
Lord Warrington	1921–1934
Lord Tomlin	1934
Lord Tomlin (died 12 August), Lord Macmillan	1935
Lord Macmillan	1936–1945
Lord Simonds	1945–1951
Sir Alan Barlow	1951–
Sir Cecil Carr	1955–1956
Rt. Hon. H. C. Montgomery Campbell	1956–1959
Sir Russell Brain, Bt.	1959–1962
M. T. Tudsbery	1962–1965
Sir Sydney Roberts	1965–1966
Sir Alan Burns	1966–1969
Lord Pearce	1969–1971
Sir Percy Faulkner	1971–1974
Sir David Pitblado	1974

Rule II – Elections

'RULE II', which has been, from the time in which we took possession of the new Club house, a special feature of the Athenaeum, has remained unchanged from the beginning, with the one exception that the words 'or for public services' were only added in the year 1848. It runs as follows:

'It being essential to the maintenance of the Athenaeum, in conformity with the principles on which it was originally founded, that the annual introduction of a certain number of persons of distinguished eminence in science, literature, or the arts, or for public services, should be secured, a limited number of persons of such qualifications shall be elected by the Committee. The number of persons so elected shall not exceed nine in each year. . . . The Club entrust this privilege to the Committee, in the entire confidence that they will only elect persons who shall have attained to distinguished eminence in science, literature, or the arts, or for public services.'

The following have been elected under the rule since 1926:-

1926
Gerard Baldwin Brown
Arthur Stanley Eddington
Maurice Greiffenhagen
Thomas Okey
George Haven Putnam
Harold J. Stiles
Burnett Hillman Streeter
Frederick Parker Walton
Fabian Ware

1927
James Berry
Sydney John Chapman
Henry Walford Davies
E. Guy Dawber
Alexander Gibb
Israel Gollancz
Frederick William Keeble
John Charles Walsham Reith
Geoffrey Ingram Taylor

1928
John Stanhope Arkwright
Edward Frankland Armstrong
William Lionel Hichens
John Blackwood McEwen
Alan Alexander Milne
Robert William Seton-Watson

1930
William Reid Dick
Robert Dixon
George Dyson
George Stuart Gordon
Harold Brewer Hartley
Allen Mawer
Owen Williams Richardson
Henry Thomas Tizard
Herbert Joseph Weld

1931
Robert Bruce

William Curtis Green
Alfred Hopkinson
Thomas Jones
Sydney Lee
Archibald Armar Montgomery-Massingberd
(Gyles) Lytton Strachey
Henry Stuart-Jones
C. Salisbury Woodward

1932
William Lawrence Bragg
George Buckston Browne
David Thomas Chadwick
Philip Guedalla
Lord Plender
Herbert Maynard Smith
Bertram Sidney Thomas
Alwyn Terrell Petre Williams
John Henry Whitley

1933
Maurice Baring
Walter Langdon Brown
Samuel Courtauld
Henry Herbert Dodwell
Harley Granville-Barker
Edmund George Valpy Knox
Ernest De Selincourt
Nevil Vincent Sidgwick
John Dover Wilson

1934
Alexander Morris Carr-Saunders
Gilbert Keith Chesterton
Arthur J. Davis
Edward Joseph Dent
William James Larke
Albert Mansbridge
Edward Mellanby
Allan Powell
Charles Leonard Woolley

1935
Harold Anson
Francis Richard Fraser
Arthur Lehman Goodhart
Lancelot Graham
Walter Hamilton Moberly
Frederick Wolff Ogilvie
George Paget Thomson
George Grey Turner

1936
Henry Balfour
Norman Hepburn Baynes
Ellie Halévy
Patrick Playfair Laidlaw
Charles Earle Raven
William Arthur Robinson
William David Ross
Stephen George Tallents

1937
Edwin John Butler
James Bryant Conant
Malcolm Baron Hailey
Warren Fisher
Ralph Howard Fowler
William Butler Yeats
Patrick Duncan
Erik Kule Palmstierna
Eustace Percy

1938
Melbourne Evans Aubrey
James Chadwick
Neville Chamberlain (Prime Minister)
Evan Charteris
Francis Lewis Castle Floud
Arthur Hinsley
John C. G. Ledingham
Richard Winn Livingstone
Viscount Nuffield

1939
William Searle Holdsworth
Lord Snell
Stanley Vernon Goodall
Harold Trevor Baker
Walter de la Mare
Frederick William Leith-Ross
Richard Bedford Bennett
John Harold Clapham
Herbert William Emerson

1940
Marquess of Lothian
Monsignor William Godfrey
J. Alfred Spender
George Russell Clerk
Henry Strakosch
Alfred Zimmern
Edwin Cooper
Henry Wood Nevinson
Hubert de la Poer Gough

1941
There was no election under Rule II in 1941.

1942
John Anderson
Dudley Pound
Archibald Wavell
Wilfrid Freeman
E. H. Minns
H. Winfield
P. M. S. Blackett
T. D. Kendrick
John Maynard Keynes

1943
Andrew Cunningham
Emile Cammaerts
W. N. Haworth
William Stanier
Thomas Lewis
Bernard Pares
Harold Raynsford Stark
Thomas James Barnes

1944
Dwight D. Eisenhower
Marquess of Linlithgow
Harlan F. Stone
Arthur Tedder
Niels Bohr
G. M. Young
C. H. Best
George Rankin
Thomas Whittemore

1945
John Gilbert Winant
Lord Catto of Cairncatto
Bennett Melvill Jones
Sydney Chapman
George Stapleton
Reginald Coupland
Samuel Eliot Morison
Stephen Gooden

1946
Viscount Alexander of Tunis
Earl of Ilchester
Viscount Montgomery of Alamein
Edward Bridges
Desmond MacCarthy
Harold Spencer Jones

1947
John Cunningham
Lord Brand
Viscount Bruce of Melbourne
Lord Vansittart

1948
Viscount Jowitt
Alexander Fleming

Oliver Franks
Marquess of Salisbury
Viscount Alanbrooke
Martin D'Arcy

1949
Lord Tovey
T. S. Eliot
Thomas K. Finletter
Arnold Toynbee
John Lowe

1950
Earl of Crawford and Balcarres
Ralph Richardson
Cameron Fromanteel Cobbold

1951
Ernest Bevin
Lord Balfour of Burleigh
William Slim
Arthur Hays Sulzberger
Viscount Weir
Ernest Gowers

1952
Lord Hankey
Lord Ismay
Earl Russell
John Rogers

1953
Earl of Halifax
Robert Sinclair

1954
R. A. Butler
Learned Hand
John Hunt
Wallace Notestein
Wilder Penfield
Lord Soulbury

1955
Edward Peacock
Lionel Charles Robbins
Jacob Epstein
Albert Edward Richardson

1956
Winston Churchill
Lester Bowles Pearson
Viscount Malvern

1957
William Keith Hancock

1958
None

1959
Vivian Fuchs

1960
Isidor Isaac Rabi
Harry Hylton-Foster

1961
Alec Guinness
Michael Knowles

1962
Eugene Black
Arthur Bliss

1963
Nil

1964
Detlev Wulf Bronk

1965
Nil

1966
Robert Menzies

1967
Nil

1968
Nil

1969
F. T. Cheng
Yehudi Menuhin

1970
William Armstrong
Humphrey Gibbs

1971
Alistair Cooke
Vincent Harris

1972
Nil

1973
Ernst Chain
Freeman Dyson
Alfred Leslie Rowse

1974
Edward Benjamin Britten
John Egerton Christmas Piper
Graham Vivian Sutherland

Index